Praise for *7 Paths to Lasting Happiness*

"Don't miss this book! If you are looking for increased personal happiness, greater productivity and satisfaction in the workplace, and more fulfilling relationships in life, *7 Paths to Lasting Happiness* is for you. Dr. Gourgouris not only lays out a roadmap to finding greater happiness, but more importantly, he provides the compass as well. This book is a gem!"

— *Captain Mike Abrashoff,*
bestselling author of It's Your Ship

"This is a really wonderful book. It contains important insights and great stories to illustrate the principles being taught. It does an especially good job in helping to close the gap between what we know and what we do. We all "know" more than what we "do." I found the book very helpful in motivating me to try to close that gap."

— *Mark Willes,*
Former CEO, Times-Mirror Corp. and Former President, General Mills.

"A superb and concise guide with specific tasks anyone can use to understand and achieve a centered life of happiness. Dr. Gourgouris presents a sensitive and scholarly book inviting us to all seek our inner desires and goals for a happy life. His professional expertise in this area is thoughtfully prepared alongside his natural empathy for all of us in search of purpose, a life of passion, and joyful relationships."

— *Raffi Minasian*
MBA Professor of Innovation and Design

"What a great book! Dr. Gourgouris does an amazing job of clearly defining the true paths to lasting happiness with his simple and practical steps. *7 Paths to Lasting Happiness* is an easy and enjoyable read, but the principles contained are timeless, profound, and incredibly valuable."

— *Terry Lyles, Ph.D.*
America's stress doctor and author of Good Stress

I have often thought that it is easier to make nice people smart than it is to make smart people nice. However, with this book Elia may have proven me wrong. During my career I have learned that a truly engaged and happy workforce will increase productivity more quickly than anything else. Dr. Gourgouris' principles can help everyone understand the key to their own happiness, and as an employer, the key to employee engagement. These 7 paths are easily followed and available to anyone - the result could very well be the personal success and happiness you have been seeking!

— Rulon F. Stacey, Ph.D,
President and CEO Fairview Health Services

"A HIT - What an informative and entertaining book! Dr. Elia Gourgouris illustrates through simple concepts and relatable stories how people can find the paths to lasting happiness within their own lives. While many seem willing to point fingers at others for impeding their happiness, Dr. Gourgouris provides a map with which one can take ownership, and, in the process, lead a happier, more fulfilling life"-

—Silva Mirzoian,
bestselling author of "Jump-Start Your Life",

7 PATHS TO LASTING HAPPINESS

7 PATHS TO LASTING HAPPINESS

Happiness is the Ultimate Success in Life!

ELIA GOURGOURIS, PH.D.
WITH JAN BENSON LINDSEY ESQ.

7 Paths to Lasting Happiness

Copyright ©2015 by Elia Gourgouris and Jan Benson Lindsey Esq.

All rights reserved, including the right to reproduce this book or portions thereof in any form whatsoever. No part of this publication may be reproduced, stored in a retrieval system, or transmitted in any form or by any means – electronic, mechanical, photocopy, recording, or any other – without the prior permission of the author.

The Happiness Center
P.O. Box 270251
Louisville CO 80027

ISBN: 978-0-9962290-0-5

Dr. Elia Gourgouris was born and raised in Athens, Greece, and at the age of eleven, he and his family moved to Santa Monica, CA. He later received his BA in psychology from UCLA, and then went on to receive both his MA and PhD in psychology.

Dr. Gourgouris, his wife, Sona, and their two sons now live near Boulder, Colorado where he enjoys spending time with his family and friends, traveling, giving service in his community, attending theater, music concerts, and movies. He enjoys nature, especially the beach, and he is a huge sports fan. When he was young he was a national swim champion in Greece.

Most of all, Dr. Gourgouris enjoys people and finds great joy in helping others transform their lives. He is the founder of The Happiness Center, an organization dedicated to helping people achieve personal success and greater happiness.

www.TheHappinessCenter.com

 Elia Gourgouris

email: DrElia@TheHappinessCenter.com

Jan Benson Lindsey Esq. grew up in Longmeadow, Massachusetts. She received her B.A. in English from Brigham Young University, and her J.D. from the J. Reuben Clark School of Law at Brigham Young University. She practiced law for thirty years before pursuing a career in writing. Ms. Lindsey and her husband Gary are the parents of three sons, and they love skiing and Jeeping in the Colorado Rockies as a family. She is also a talented musician.

Dedication

To my parents, who taught me how to love!

Acknowledgments

I am deeply indebted to so many people who inspired me to write this book. First and foremost I would like to express my love and appreciation to Sona, my best friend and companion over the last 25 years. She has been my inspiration and I am a better man when I'm in her presence. Thank you for always believing in me and for your continuous support throughout this wonderful journey. Thank you to my boys Niko and Dimitri for keeping me young and laughing! Thank you to my older brother Stathi who's always been so loving and such a great example and to my late dad Thimio, for sacrificing so much to bring us to America.

A big thank you to Jan Benson Lindsey Esq. for the countless hours we spent together crafting this marvelous book. I am so grateful we took this journey together...Thank you for pushing me to make this the very best book possible. I could not have done this without you, my friend!

Many thanks to Chris Snelgrove for your invaluable assistance with navigating the twists and turns of the publishing process. Your professionalism and generosity in sharing your knowledge are greatly appreciated.

A very special thank you to Nick Taylor for the beautiful book cover design. You are the consummate professional and a pleasure to work with.

Finally, to my beautiful late mother Petrula who taught me to love unconditionally and whose parting words to me were, "I just want you to be happy!"

I dedicate this book to all who are striving to find and to spread happiness to those around them.

— Elia Gourgouris Ph.D.

June 2015

Contents

Dedication viii
Acknowledgments ix
Introduction 13
Chapter One: Happiness is a Choice! 17
Chapter Two: Let's Get Started! 31
Chapter Three: The First Path: Love Yourself (Part 1) 47
Chapter Four: The First Path: Love Yourself (Part 2) 63
Chapter Five: The Second Path: Be Grateful 85
Chapter Six: The Third Path: Extend Forgiveness 109
Chapter Seven: The Fourth Path: Follow Your Passion 131
Chapter Eight: The Fifth Path: Nourish Your Spirit 159
Chapter Nine: The Sixth Path: Create Loving Relationships 177
Chapter Ten: The Seventh Path: Serve From Your Heart 217
Conclusion 245
Chapter Notes 249

Introduction

"Happiness is the meaning and the purpose of life, the whole aim and end of human existence."
—*Aristotle*

BEING HAPPY EVERY DAY IS ACHIEVABLE! I'M NOT TALKING ABOUT superficial happiness but about deep down, *lasting* happiness.

As a professional psychologist, executive coach and life coach, for over 25 years I have worked with thousands of people, ranging from highly successful corporate leaders to young teenagers. I have counseled people struggling with addictions, depression, self-destructive behaviors, low self-esteem, relationship issues, self-defeating thoughts and other challenges. Despite their widely varying circumstances, I have learned from my clients that certain principles are universal to our quest for long-term happiness.

The concepts discussed in this book are derived from my years of work experience, and they are not theories. They are practical, time-tested principles that have been proven to make a difference. Over the years, as I have stayed in touch with many clients, I have seen the positive changes that have happened in their personal, family and professional lives. If you apply these principles in your own life, it has been my experience that you too can achieve real happiness!

As you begin this life-enhancing journey toward lasting happiness, you will probably discover you need to make a few changes in your life. For one, you may need to rethink some of your attitudes about the sources of happiness. Taking a fresh look at what you believe can open up a world of possibilities. Ultimately, happiness boils down to small course corrections made daily. They will lead you to becoming a happier person.

Most self-help books have wonderful ideas and inspiring concepts. But what usually happens after we read a book like that? If we only read it, highlight a few things, and put it away on a shelf when we're finished, then very little will change. If that's the kind of book you're looking for, *this isn't it*.

I know many people who are knowledgeable and highly educated, yet who are quite unhappy in their lives. They know intellectually the steps to happiness, **but knowledge without application is just education.** I can read the top 10 books on how to become a millionaire, and underline and highlight them to death. If I don't *act* upon what they say, I'll still be in the same financial position I was in before I read them, just more knowledgeable.

It's the same way with happiness. You can learn all the things that contribute to true, lasting happiness, like gratitude, forgiveness and love, but if you don't *apply* them in your life *on a daily basis*, not much will change.

This book is really about undergoing a transformation at a much deeper level. The only way for any of us to make a real change is to become personally involved in the process. Just reading might present some new ideas, but thinking through and *applying* those ideas into our own lives can truly transform us.

The most effective way to read this book is to read it slowly and thoughtfully, perhaps one chapter a week. There is an Action Section at the end of each chapter, which includes Points to Ponder, Questions to Consider, and Action Steps for you to take. Reflect upon the Points to Ponder and the Questions to Consider, and then *take the Action Steps*! Once you begin to actually take action, the changes you desire in your life will automatically follow!

The difference between who you are and who you want to be is what you do! If happiness is what you seek, then reading, pondering, and applying *7 Paths to Lasting Happiness* is a great way to start! Let the journey begin!

— *Dr. Elia Gourgouris*

Your life does not get better by chance, it gets better by change.
—Jim Rohn

Chapter One
Happiness is a Choice!

"No one is in charge of your happiness. Except you."
—*Unknown*

THE GOOD NEWS IS, WE CAN *CONTROL* WHETHER WE ARE HAPPY! Although much of our natural disposition for happiness is based on our genetic makeup[1], and therefore varies from person to person, it is merely an inherited tendency, not our destiny[*]. Our destiny is, and always will be, what we work toward, what we accomplish in our lives.

Happiness expert Sonja Lyubomirsky, a professor of psychology at the University of California-Riverside, compared the genetically determined happiness "set point" to our inherited tendency to stay thin or to put on weight. She believes that

---
[*] The late David Lykken, a behavioral geneticist and Professor Emeritus of Psychology and Psychiatry at the University of Minnesota, conducted 30 years of research on twins – much of it on identical twins who were raised apart. He found that 50% of our proclivity for happiness or for melancholy (our "set point") is determined by our genes.[2]

> "All the set point means is that in the same way some people have to work on maintaining their weight, [a person] may have to work to achieve the same level of happiness as someone else. It may be harder, but it can be done."[3]

So if we're not as happy as we'd like to be - we *can* do something about it. And that's the purpose of this book: to lead you to discover the process of how you can become happy.

What Is Happiness, Anyway?

As Aristotle said, "Happiness is the meaning and the purpose of life, the whole aim . . . of human existence." One of the greatest achievements we can attain in life is leaving this world a better place than we found it. If we're in a perpetual state of despair, how can we make the world better? How will our lives have meaning, either to ourselves or to others?

Almost every day of our lives, somebody will ask, "How are you?" And unless it's a very close friend or family member, our response is usually, "I'm fine." My Greek father thought this was very strange when we first moved to the United States. "How can everybody be fine?!" he would exclaim. "Everybody you come across, every day, they say they're fine – *that's not possible*! There's no way everybody's *fine* all the time!" In contrast, in Greece people will tell anyone who asks them, *exactly* how they are doing. (Sometimes they provide a little *too much* information!)

> *The greatest part of our happiness depends on our dispositions, not our circumstances.*
> —Martha Washington

What does being happy feel like? Do we recognize happiness when we are experiencing it? It is a sustainable sense of spiritual contentment that arises from deep within. It is a condition of the heart. It is not giddiness, silliness, or ecstasy. What many people don't realize, though, is that happiness is the result of a decision made (whether consciously or unconsciously), to *be* happy. Of course, most people prefer to believe that their unhappiness is due to their circumstances, not because of a choice they've made. But if our happiness were dependent on our circumstances, people would rarely be happy, because no one has a perfect, pain-free life. We all experience challenges, hardships, adversity, and disappointments. It's a part of human existence.

The way we interpret the world we see will in large measure determine our "happiness quotient." The power is *within us* right now to be happy, independent of our circumstances. Elizabeth Gilbert put it well in her bestselling novel, *Eat, Pray, Love*:

> I keep remembering one of my Guru's teachings about happiness. She says that people universally tend to think that happiness is a stroke of luck, something that will maybe descend upon you like fine weather if you're fortunate enough. But that's not how happiness works. **Happiness is the consequence of personal effort.** You fight for it, strive for it, insist upon it . . . You have to participate relentlessly in the manifestations of your own blessings. And once you have achieved a state of happiness, **you must never become lax about maintaining it**, you must make a mighty effort to keep swimming upward into that happiness forever, to stay afloat on top of

it. If you don't, you will leak away your innate contentment. It's easy enough to pray when you're in distress but continuing to pray even when your crisis has passed is like a sealing process, helping your soul hold tight to its good attainments.[4] [Emphasis added]

Dr. Viktor Frankl, the bestselling author of *Man's Search for Meaning* and a renowned Austrian psychiatrist, survived the holocaust in Germany. While watching his fellow inmates in a Nazi concentration camp, he observed that all things could be taken from a man *except the final freedom: the ability to choose how he will respond to any situation*. When my wife Sona and I visited the Auschwitz concentration camp where Dr. Frankl was an inmate, the strength of the human spirit and the profound truth of his observations struck me with stunning force.

It was a cool, cloudy day in May of 1995. The dark weather reflected the mood inside the camp. It was quiet, solemn, and very few people were on the grounds. We walked alone, quietly, through the compound as we viewed rooms, walled off by plexi-glass that gave a glimpse into the horrifying reality of what Auschwitz was. The first chamber we passed overflowed with a mountain of shoes – thousands of them – left behind as their owners were herded to their executions; the next contained a ceiling-high pile of their suitcases, abandoned at the command of their captors; another held countless pairs of eyeglasses; the next, a heart-rending mound of children's and babies' shoes. The worst room was the last – it contained large heaps of human hair, shaved from the heads of the doomed prisoners. Final was the execution wall, where the hapless victims were shot. It was filled with countless bullet holes. We had only been there for an hour, but the darkness and complete despair of the place overwhelmed both of us and we had to leave. We drove all the way to Berlin – a long drive – without saying a word to one another.

We visited Auschwitz 50 years after its heinous operations had been halted by the Allied troops. I walked through as a free man, with no guns pointed at me. I hadn't had any loved ones killed or taken from me; I hadn't lost everything I owned in the world; and even so, I couldn't handle more than an hour in that place. It was in this terrible hell-on-earth that Viktor Frankl kept his spirit, and the spirits of many other inmates, alive. He realized that we all have the ability to choose how we will respond to any situation. It is the power of choice that determines much of how we feel, every day of our lives.

> *Most folks are about as happy as they make up their mind to be.*
> —Abraham Lincoln

The following story is a great example of somebody who decided in advance to be content in "whatsoever state he was:"

> A 92 year-old, poised and proud man was fully dressed each morning by eight o'clock, with his hair fashionably combed and shaved perfectly, even though he was legally blind. When his wife of 70 years passed away, he had to move to a nursing home. After many hours of waiting patiently in the lobby of the nursing home, he smiled sweetly when told his room was ready. As he maneuvered his walker to the elevator, the nurse accompanying him provided a visual description of his tiny room, including the eyelet curtains that had been hung on his window.

"I love it!" he exclaimed, with the enthusiasm of an 8-year-old who has just been presented with a new puppy.

"Mr. Jones, you haven't seen the room; just wait."

"That doesn't have anything to do with it," he replied. "Happiness is something you decide on ahead of time. Whether I like my room or not doesn't depend on how the furniture is arranged. It's how I arrange my mind. I already decided to love it. It's a decision I make every morning when I wake up. I have a choice: I can spend the day in bed recounting the difficulty I have with the parts of my body that no longer work, or get out of bed and be thankful for the ones that do. Each day is a gift, and as long as my eyes open, I'll focus on the new day and all the happy memories I've stored away - just for this time in my life. Old age is like a bank account. You withdraw from what you've put in. So, my advice to you would be to deposit a lot of happiness in the bank account of memories!"

—*Author unknown*

Of course, anyone can choose to be *un*happy. But who in their right mind would choose to be unhappy? Life would seem pretty pointless! Nevertheless, the power of choice exists in every circumstance, for each of us.

Is Happiness Worth the Effort?

If it takes an effort to be happy, why try? Is happiness worth the effort? There are lots of reasons that life is more fulfilling when we're happy. Being happy or seeking after happiness doesn't mean one is selfish; to be happy is essential and life sustaining. Our happiness, or lack thereof, influences our daily interactions and *all* of our relationships with others. If we're happy, it will bless our spouse, our children, our neighbors and friends, and our co-workers. The world is a better place when the happiest version of us is walking around. While it can require work, there's no doubt that being happy is worth the effort. Following are some of the reasons happiness is worth the effort:

> **The world is a better place when the happiest version of us is walking around.**

1) Happiness is Success. Common sense has always dictated that happy people live longer, enjoy healthier lives, maintain better relationships, and are more successful than chronically unhappy people. Modern research studies have confirmed that. According to Ed Diener, professor of psychology at the University of Illinois, "This doesn't mean that people need to be euphoric or ecstatic all the time, but rather that people who are in a positive state the majority of the time have an advantage in terms of success."[5]

A friend once told me, "Success is happiness." I thought about this comment for a minute as I reflected on the many so-called successful people I had worked with in my practice. They were all seeking personal contentment and fulfillment, which had eluded them. A lot of those "successful" people were downright miserable. Despite their huge careers, they had broken-down relationships, addictions, and other sad reasons they had come to me for help. Over and over I heard the plaintive phrase, "There's something missing from my life!" My work with these people led me to the realization that true success is achieving happiness, not the other way around. And I turned to my friend and responded, "No, happiness is success!"

Given the choice, would one rather buy a car from a grumpy salesperson, or a warm and friendly salesperson? Even if it means paying a few more dollars, most people would prefer dealing with the happy person. We tend to project virtues onto happy people. They appear to us to be smarter, more genuine, even more honest and fair.

> *Success is not the key to happiness. Happiness is the key to success. If you love what you are doing, you will be successful.*
> —Albert Schweitzer

2) Happiness is Healthy. We've all known (at least subconsciously) since we were kids that happiness is healthy. Our stomachs feel awful when we're sad, angry, worried, or afraid. Imagine how a negative state of mind must affect the other systems in our bodies!

A Norwegian medical researcher reported recently that adults who have a sense of humor outlive those who can't find anything funny about life. Sven Svebak of the medical school at Norwegian University of Science and Technology studied a group of 54,000 individuals for seven years and found that those who maintained a sense of humor, even when facing the gloomiest of personal situations, tended to live longer. According to Svebak's research, humor cut the chances of death for cancer patients by 70%.[6]

My friend Jan battled Non-Hodgkin Lymphoma twenty years ago. As she underwent chemotherapy for the second year in a row, her immune system got weaker and weaker. Typically, she'd have her blood levels checked on a Friday, and if everything was all right, she'd go to the hospital the following Monday to get the next round of chemotherapy. On the Friday before she was supposed to get her 6th dose of chemotherapy, the doctor told her that her white blood cell count was simply too low, so she wouldn't be able to get chemo that next week. The doctor didn't know that Jan was on a schedule of her own! She had to stay on track with the chemotherapy schedule in order to be able to go on a San Juan Islands sailing trip 3 months later. The anticipation of that sailing trip was helping her get through the many days of nausea and weakness.

Jan had heard that laughter has been clinically proven to increase a person's white blood cell count. Unwilling to accept the doctor's verdict, on the way home she asked her husband to rent some funny movies. She watched them all, and spent a significant part of the weekend laughing. The following Monday morning, she returned to the doctor's office to have her white blood cell count re-checked. To the doctor's amazement, the count was high enough for Jan to be able to check into the hospital and start the next dose of chemo. This same scenario repeated itself for the three remaining cycles of chemotherapy that she had to endure, so she was able to stay on schedule and go on the sailing trip.

Despite predictions by her doctors that Jan would not survive more than a few more months, she is still alive and well, more than twenty years later. She's living proof that being happy can help us be healthier.

3) Happiness is Being Connected to Other People. When you need advice from a friend, do you go to somebody who's happy, or to somebody who is full of despair? People tend to go to those who are happy when they seek advice, ideas, or comfort. Unhappy people often have a negative energy that sends the message, "Keep out – stay away." When a person feels like nobody loves them, the message they often unconsciously send to others is, "Keep your distance." Then others respond to that message and DO keep their distance. Sadly, the unhappy person usually doesn't see their part in it – they only see the outcome. People stay away from them, so their interpretation is, "I'm unlovable; nobody wants to be with me, and nobody wants to spend time with me." They don't understand that others are just responding to their non-verbal social cues.

Similarly, people will respond in a *happy* way to *positive* non-verbal social cues. In January of 2010, a colleague of mine - Dr. Terry Lyles - and I went on a humanitarian mission to Haiti. A massive earthquake had rocked the country, and as we walked the streets of Port-Au-Prince, the faces of the Haitian people were very somber. Almost nobody smiled. Many were homeless or had lost loved ones, and despair was everywhere. What struck me, however, was that every time I made eye contact, smiled and said, "Bonjour! Comment allez-vous?" ("Hi! How are you?") people would light up and respond with a smile. The result was a complete change in the energy of the situation.

> *Thousands of candles can be lighted from a single candle, and the life of the candle will not be shortened. Happiness never decreases by being shared.*
> —**Buddha**

If I want to change the world, it has to start with me. If I want to have a positive environment around me, I have to contribute to that. If my contribution is a smile, a polite gesture, or something welcoming, the majority of people will respond with kindness and warmth. If I'm angry or unkind, I'm probably going to get that back in return. The fact is, my contribution is the only thing I can control.

The fact is, my contribution is the only thing I can control.

I have no power over any other person's mood, but I may have some influence on them by sending some kindness and warmth their way.

> *Every time you smile at someone, it is an action of love,*
> *a gift to that person, a beautiful thing.*
> —**Mother Teresa**

The bottom line is, if you want to be connected to other people, to have rewarding relationships, you need to be happy at least *some* of the time.

4) **Happiness is Attractive.** It's undeniable—happiness is attractive! A smile reveals warmth emanating from deep within. Everyone is attracted to that. Being happy communicates "I am healthy, connected, powerful, motivated, and have direction and purpose in my life." It is rare that all these elements are working together for us at one time. But if we appear to be happy, our lives radiate warmth and people are drawn to us.

Our happiness depends on the way we live our lives and how we view the world.

Our happiness depends on the way we live our lives and how we view the world.

The True Source of Happiness

Many myths exist about what constitutes true happiness. The media continually presents us with insinuations that a fit body, dazzling white teeth, wealth, power, fame, or possessions, lead to happiness. Pleasure, which is short-lived, is frequently portrayed as being the same thing as happiness. Not that there's anything wrong with pleasure! It's a wonderful part of being alive, but it should not be mistaken for true and lasting happiness.

Some people erroneously believe happiness is an absence of the trials that are a natural part of living on this earth. They feel that if only they had no pain, losses, disappointments, or illnesses, then they would be truly happy. Instead of seeing life's obstacles as opportunities for growth, they begin to view challenges as stumbling blocks designed to impede their personal happiness.

The real solution lies within each of us. **Our happiness depends on the way we live our lives and how we view the world.** We each create the lens through which we view the world. We can each change that lens and discover the true sources of happiness by incorporating into our lives the seven principles discussed in this book. The process described in the following chapters will teach you the true sources of happiness – and more importantly, *how* **to be happy.**

> *Being happy doesn't mean that everything is perfect.*
> *It means you've decided to look beyond the imperfections.*
> —**Unknown**

Points to ponder:
1. Happiness is a choice.
2. Happiness is success!
3. Happiness is attractive!

Questions to consider:
1. Are you ready to be happy?
2. How willing are you to take the steps necessary to be happy?

Take Action

Where have you sought happiness in the past? List five areas where you've sought happiness in the past. (Some examples might be money, material possessions, travel, relationships with people, and even drugs.)

1. _____
2. _____
3. _____
4. _____
5. _____

Now briefly describe the results of seeking happiness in each of those five areas. To what degree did you find true happiness (as opposed to pleasure)? Completely, somewhat, or not at all?

1. _____
2. _____
3. _____
4. _____
5. _____

Chapter Two

Let's Get Started!

*"If you pile up too many tomorrows, you'll end up with
a lot of empty yesterdays."*
—Unknown

IF YOU WANT TO BE HAPPY, IT'S TIME TO GET GOING. WHEN I WAS YOUNG, my Uncle Dimitrios used to take my brother and me to the Long Beach Grand Prix in California. It was a wondrous experience I'll never forget.

> **Mending the holes in our heart and in our conscience demand immediate attention.**

I decided that the phrase "Gentlemen, start your engines" was one of the most thrilling in the English language. The anticipation and the roar of all the fired-up horsepower were almost too much to bear, as we waited for the flag to drop! But what if it had never dropped? What if all those supercharged, revved-up, powerful machines had just sat there, racing their engines and blowing through many gallons of high-octane fuel? What would have been the point?

Finding happiness is urgent! Our well-being depends on it. It is not like some random fix-it project that can be put off. Mending the hole in the basement wall can be postponed indefinitely; but mending the holes in our heart and in our conscience demand immediate attention. Our potential for success, wealth, influence and loving relationships are all hampered, if we're not happy. Our ability to contribute in a meaningful way to others – whether they are family members, associates at work, or the community we live in – is weakened if we're not happy. And perhaps most significantly, if we're not happy, we don't fully benefit from the relationships, success, and love we already have in our lives. It takes a commitment, but the time to be happy is *now*! So let's get started!

> *Happiness is not an accident. Nor is it something you wish for. Happiness is something you design.*
> —Jim Rohn

Change is Good for Us

We all have the opportunity to change our thinking and behavior. At first, it may be uncomfortable. Even though change is the only constant in life, human nature is notorious for resisting change - almost at all costs. We are creatures of habit. We like the familiar, even if it's dysfunctional. I've worked with people who are unhappy, who are in dysfunctional relationships, and yet they're ambivalent about change. They're afraid to make a change because the result is unknown. They're afraid of experiencing something new, even if it might improve their lives. They exemplify the old adage, "The evil we know is safer than the evil we don't know."

Everybody remembers the time when they first learned how to drive a car. The prospect of the freedom that driving would bring was exhilarating and life-changing! But the mechanics of controlling a several-thousand pound car is not second nature to most people. It took practice to learn how much to depress the accelerator, how hard to step on the brake, how to safely change lanes, how to merge into traffic on a busy road, and all the other skills we had to develop. If you were like me, that time of learning involved some pretty uncomfortable, sometimes even terrifying, moments. But once the skills were developed and mastered, driving became second nature. The freedom it brought felt miraculous.

Similarly, changing our thinking and behavior to be happy may feel uncomfortable or unfamiliar at first. But once we develop the skills to be happy, the freedom that happiness brings will also feel miraculous.

It starts with a dream.
Add faith,
and it becomes a belief,
Add action,
and it becomes a part of life.
Add perseverance,
and it becomes a goal in sight.
Add patience and time,
and it ends
with a dream come true.
—Doe Zantamata

Fuel for Change

Do you really want to be happy? Or is it easier just to remain unhappy? It's your choice. The status quo, even an unhappy one, may seem less threatening than making significant changes that alter life patterns. If the prospect of change is so unpleasant, what motivates us to change? Significant change is usually fueled by specific feelings, some of which create a sense of urgency. Sometimes we don't change until the pain of our current choices overwhelms the perceived pleasure or benefit we are deriving from our current choices.

Of course, not all changes are good. But change of any kind in our lives deserves a second look. What makes us move, act, or change? What creates a sense of urgency, makes us get up and get going? For most people, the motivation can be traced to pain, anger, fear, duty/responsibility or love.

1) Pain. Some people will make a change in their lives because the current condition is causing too much pain. Take the example of an addict: when he hits rock bottom, it's usually with such a thud that everyone can hear it. The physical, emotional, and spiritual gas tanks are empty and there's not another service station around for miles. The pain is so piercing and pervasive that it seems like no relief is possible. Family members are at their own rock bottoms and often can provide no help or support until the addict finally seeks sobriety. Some alcoholics who want to escape the pain simply end their lives. For others, the abandonment, loss, and physical turbulence motivate them to reach within and find the capacity to break the addiction cycle. But we don't *have* to wait until we're in crazy, rock-bottom pain to make a change!

When I have worked with addicts, I ask them, "Do you have to wait until you've lost your job, your husband/wife, your family, *everything*, or can you make the change *now*?" Clearly they were asking for help, or they wouldn't have been seeing me. Change made to escape pain is good, as long as a positive course of action is chosen.

2) Anger. Some people make changes because of anger. The frustration, anger, and sense of loss felt by a spouse who has been betrayed are difficult to describe to anyone who has not experienced it. The rage seems to boil up inside and spill out as anger at others, self, and even God. It's often best to give oneself a "time-out" to collect one's thoughts, rather than to make a hasty decision while angry. Decisions made while a person is in an highly emotional state may be unwise.

3) Fear. Fear can generate paralysis, which keeps us from moving forward, but it can also be a motivating emotion. When considering the impact of a life-threatening illness, major financial crisis, career setback, or crumbling marriage vows, fear may push us to take action. Unfortunately, actions based on fear are frequently made with only short-term gains in mind, which may be counter-productive in the long run. When change is motivated by fear, it may result in a hasty and under-informed decision.

4) Duty. When we do something due to a sense of duty, we do it because it's what we're supposed to do, because of a responsibility we have accepted. An example would be working to support our family. There's nothing wrong with having duty as a motivator; often a sense of duty propels us to take action. It's a more positive motivator than pain, anger, or fear, especially if we act without resentment. It's not as uplifting as acting out of love, but often when we act out of a sense of duty, it can change to love.

5) Love. The "highest power" to effect change is love. True affection for another, or the desire to be a blessing to others, motivates a true and lasting change of behavior on the part of the one who loves. And don't overlook that this includes loving yourself!

My mother was an example of bringing about change through love. When she died of cancer, her loss was devastating to me. I was only 22, but her parting words to me have had a powerful impact on me for the rest of my life. She said, "Don't worry about me, I'll be fine! I just want you to be happy!" That was the last thing I ever heard from my mom.

One of the most remarkable things my mother taught me was to love everyone unconditionally, to never judge, to always give the benefit of the doubt, and to live life to the fullest (which she had done, even after her cancer had returned a second, and finally a third, time). After she spoke those final words, I was more determined than ever before to live the way she had taught me to live.

What's your motivator?

Having listed some of the most common motivators for change, consider what's going to motivate *you* to change to become happy. What's making you *un*happy? Is your life full of pain? Are you angry or fearful because of your current situation? Do you feel a responsibility that makes you want to choose something different? Maybe it's all of the above. Perhaps you want to change because of love. How about making a change because you love *yourself*? Whatever your motivator may be, *I promise you* that making a change to be happy will be liberating!

Are You an Optimist or a Pessimist?

A pessimist sees the difficulty in every opportunity;
an optimist sees the opportunity in every difficulty.
— **Sir Winston Churchill**

As we grow up and learn from those around us, and as we experience the events that occur in our lives, we may allow the lens through which we view the world to become warped - too focused on the negative. Do you see the glass half full, or half empty? What is the real difference between being an optimist vs. being a pessimist? There's an anecdote that illustrates the point well: the optimist wakes up every morning, looks out the window and says "Good morning, God!" Before anything else takes place, there's an acknowledgement and expression of gratitude to start off the day. The pessimist wakes up the same morning, looks out the same window and declares, "Good God, it's morning!" Clearly, nothing bad has transpired yet, but there's already lament for the new day ahead.

So the day begins and they're both wearing their expectations on their sleeves. Everything that will take place during the day will be viewed through their unique lens. Imagine the following example: both the optimist and the pessimist get a flat tire on the way to work as they're exiting the freeway, but they have different reactions. The optimist counts his blessings because the flat happened as the car was slowing down on the exit ramp, and not while it was traveling on the freeway at 70 miles per hour. Gratitude fills his heart for being so fortunate! The pessimist pulls over, inspects the flat tire and thinks to himself, "Why do these things *always* happen to me? Now I'll be late for work and my boss will probably fire me!"

People who are pessimists ask questions like, "What's wrong with my life . . . my parents . . . my kids . . . my spouse?" Anybody who *actually asks* those questions out loud will get very long responses, especially to that last one! When negative questions are asked, negativity rules! But if we ask positive questions instead, such as

- "What am I grateful for?"
- "Who loves me?"
- "What's great about my family?"
- "What can I do today to make someone happy?" or
- "What do I admire about my husband/wife?"

Then the focus of the lens through which we view life will change, and we can become an optimist.

What's your "brand?"

How does a person end up as either an optimist or a pessimist? I can tell you from personal experience that it can start early on in life. I was born a long time ago, in Greece. Back then, nobody was allowed in the birthing room. So when my dad showed up at the hospital after I was born, he approached a nurse and asked to see his son. The nurse took him to the nursery window, where 5 babies were bundled in identical little white blankets. He asked which one was his son. At that particular moment I was gurgling cheerfully, so the nurse pointed at me and responded, "HE'S THE HAPPY ONE!"

From that day on I was branded the "happy one," as the story was told over and over again in my youth. For those who know me well, it truly has been my "nature" or disposition for the most part throughout my life. The question then becomes, was I *really* born that way, or was it being told or "branded" as being happy that made me assume that role? What if my dad had gotten stuck in traffic and was a few minutes late? By the time he got to the hospital to ask the nurse the same question, I might have been having a stomachache and screaming my head off. The nurse could easily have turned to him and said, "HE'S THE FUSSY ONE!" If that had been the case, I might have been told that I was born fussy, and have been cranky ever since!

A friend of mine was labeled early on by her parents as the "peacemaker" of the family. In a family of four children who were close to one another in age, trivial spats and disagreements easily broke out among the siblings. After having heard herself referred to as the "peacemaker" by her parents on more than one occasion, she felt a responsibility to live up to that brand. Even if it hadn't been said for a long time, whenever an argument occurred, she heard the words "the peacemaker" resounding in her memory, and she would respond accordingly, trying to diffuse a fight.

So here's a question for you: what is *your* brand? We all have one, whether it's happy, cranky, smart, cute, hyperactive, artistic, dirty, creative, fat, ugly, stupid, or something else. Whatever it is, if you like your brand, then count your blessings, and keep it forever! If, however, you don't like it, today is a new day and you can replace it with a new brand. A brand that you *love*!

I'll always remember a woman I met while addressing a conference as a keynote speaker in North Carolina. As I talked about branding and how we may be stuck with labels we don't care for, she raised her hand and commented, "I don't like my brand." This lady was middle-aged, and she had lived with her brand for a very long time. She didn't want to live with it for the rest of her life. I asked her, "From now on, what do you want your brand to be?"

Her lighthearted answer was, "I want to be Princess so-and-so!" My immediate response was, "OKAY, your majesty!" and everyone in the audience laughed, which left her smiling. Right then and there, she was taking an important step: it was the beginning of a whole new, positive attitude in life for her. She made a conscious decision to no longer allow the invalid, negative brand be a part of her self-image. Eleanor Roosevelt summed up this principle quite succinctly when she said, "No one can make you feel inferior without your consent."[1]

When I was 14, I saw a more contemporary illustration of this truth. The Reverend Jesse Jackson was on television, talking to an auditorium full of disadvantaged kids who were on the periphery of society. He taught them a new mantra: "Nobody – but NOBODY – can tell me I'm nobody!" He had them say it over and over again, getting louder each time. It's a great message – and a true one: nobody can tell us we're nobody – unless we *allow* them to.

You may have to do some internal searching to figure out how you were branded earlier in your life. If we recognize the messages of discontent we are repeating to ourselves, we have a really good chance of diminishing or even completely eliminating their effect. If you don't like your brand, adopt one you love. Tell your family and friends about your newfound identity: "Just call me Princess from now on and nobody gets hurt!" Believe it or not, the beginning of change really could be that simple.

Getting Started

I believe that most people truly want to be happy and to have rewarding relationships with others. They want to thrive – not just survive – but they don't know *how*. Learning how to be happy is an essential life skill that not all of us learned in childhood. This book is the road map for a way to develop that skill.

The principles discussed in the following chapters will show you true sources of happiness, a way to live more happily, and they can help you refocus the lens through which you view life. They constitute *7 Paths to Lasting Happiness*. As you read each chapter, take time to reflect upon the Points to Ponder, the Questions to Consider, and most importantly, **do** the action steps in the Take Action Section. Follow each Path, and incorporate its principles into your life until it becomes a habit before moving on to the next chapter.

I know from my personal experience that if we practice these principles until they become daily habits, we *will* be happier. And that's a promise!

Points to ponder:

I can control my thoughts, my attitude, and the way I view life.

Questions to consider:

1. What am I willing to do today, to have a better tomorrow?

2. If I start right now, where will I be in a year, as opposed to just letting the status quo continue?

Take Action

Respond to the questions in the following Life Satisfaction Survey. The insights learned will give you an indication of how happy you feel on your current life's path. Responding to the survey should take a maximum of 5 minutes.

Life Satisfaction Survey[2]

Please answer the following questions, using the criteria below. Please choose the number which most closely fits how you feel at this time in your life, and write it in the box to the right of the question:
- **0** - Never feel this way
- **1** - Rarely feel this way
- **2** - Sometimes feel this way
- **3** - Often feel this way
- **4** - Always feel this way

	- 1 - 2 - 3 - 4 -
1) I know what my purpose in life is.	
2) I am excited about learning new things and developing my skills and talents.	
3) My life is in balance physically	
4) My life is in balance emotionally.	
5) My life is in balance spiritually.	
6) When life feels "out of control," I choose healthy behaviors to help me re-center and renew. (i.e. I do not use shopping, eating, sleeping, television / internet, or other substances to escape and cope).	
7) I am aware and enjoy living in the moment (I don't dwell on future or past events).	
8) I have fulfilling relationships with family and friends.	
9) I have fulfilling intimate relationships in my life.	
10) Humor, laughter, and playfulness are a big part of my daily life.	
11) My partnerships are fairly and equally balanced (work and personal).	

	- 1 - 2 - 3 - 4 -
12) I find positive ways to deal with stress. (i.e. exercise, talking, meditating, etc).	
13) I exercise appropriate control over the things that I can in my life.	
14) I live life with an attitude of gratitude.	
15) I live my life with passion and joy.	
16) I have exciting dreams and aspirations to look forward to.	
17) I am an optimistic person.	
18) I enjoy hearing other people's insights and points of view, even when they are different from my own.	
19) I find it easy to forgive others when I have been hurt.	
20) I apologize and make amends quickly when I have hurt someone else.	
21) I am good at keeping events in my life in perspective.	
22) I live with integrity and honesty in all my dealings.	
23) Kindness and compassion are virtues that I practice daily.	
24) I perform acts of service daily.	
25) I have a strong faith which sustains me throughout my life.	

Next step: Calculate your score

Assign the following points to your answers to the questions:
- **0** points for each "Never" response.
- **1** point for each "Rarely" response.
- **2** points for each "Sometimes" response.
- **3** points for each "Often" response.
- **4** points for each "Always" response.

Add all of the points together to calculate your total score and then write it here:

Interpreting your score:

There are two ways to interpret your score. The first is your cumulative score, which gives you an indication of your overall sense of fulfillment and happiness in life:

81-100: I am generally contented and happy in my life. Feedback in specific areas might be useful.

61-80: My life is okay, but not always what I would like it to be. I could use some direction in making my life happier.

41-60: My life is not going in a direction I would like it to go. I need guidance in learning how to find happiness.

40 and Under: My life lacks fulfillment and joy. (Don't give up – this is a great opportunity for growth!)

The second way to interpret your score has to do with the individual areas which are covered in the survey. Research has shown that the twenty-five areas addressed in the questions are specific indicators which contribute to one's overall sense of happiness. So, for example, if a score was less than four on a particular question, it shows room for improvement *in that specific area*. The lower the score, the greater the opportunity for growth.

Chapter Three

The First Path: Love Yourself
Part 1 - Recognizing Your Worth

"If we really love ourselves, everything in our life works."
—*Louise L. Hay*

LOVING ONESELF IS THE FOUNDATION OF PERSONAL HAPPINESS. IT'S ALSO the greatest gift we can give ourselves. The lack of it can be devastating. People with addictions, self-defeating thoughts and self-destructive behaviors have something in common: deep down inside, they lack love for themselves.

> When we take care of ourselves, we are choosing to love ourselves.

People who are truly happy, on the other hand, recognize their value and have a strong sense of self-worth. They don't want to hurt themselves by engaging in self-defeating thoughts like negative thinking, or self-destructive actions like snorting cocaine, or drinking to excess. A natural byproduct of taking care of ourselves is that we won't adopt damaging behaviors. When we take care of ourselves, we are choosing to love ourselves. An important part of loving ourselves is not comparing ourselves to others.

The Risk of Comparisons

The importance of eliminating or limiting the toxic relationships in our lives is discussed in Chapter Nine. That includes having a healthy relationship with *ourselves*. How do people get to the point that they no longer love themselves? Frequently, it's because they compare themselves to everyone around them. In the Bible, Jesus said, "Judge not, that ye be not judged." (Matthew 7:1 Authorized King James Version). In essence, He may as well have been saying, "You should not compare!" Every time you compare yourself to another person, there are only two possible outcomes:

1. Either you'll decide "I'm better than you are," and then you're guilty of being arrogant and prideful, or
2. You'll conclude, "You're better than I am," which makes you feel bad about yourself - like you're not good enough.

Most people engage in such comparisons, and frequently with unpleasant results. Who doesn't know an arrogant person who thinks he's better than everybody else? Ironically, this kind of behavior actually stems from insecurity. A person who brags has a little voice inside himself saying, "I'm not good enough – I have to prove myself."

A friend of mine who is an attorney worked for one of the biggest law firms in the country. She told me an interesting story about an elevator ride she once took with the firm's managing partner.

She had never met him before, and as they rode from the 1st floor to the 22nd floor together, she introduced herself. He immediately announced that he was a graduate of the Harvard Law School. My friend responded by telling the partner a little bit about herself, but he cut her off and announced again that he was a graduate of the Harvard Law School! When my friend *still* didn't respond with what the partner deemed to be the appropriate amount of awe, he announced it again! The elevator ride really wasn't all that long – probably about 50-60 seconds - but between the 1st and the 22nd floors, he mentioned *three* times that he had graduated from Harvard! Unable to stand hearing it a fourth time, my friend finally delivered the compliment the partner was fishing for and confirmed that graduating from the Harvard Law School was an extremely impressive accomplishment! She got off the elevator with the impression that the managing partner of one of the biggest law firms in the country was an extremely insecure man. He had accomplished exactly the opposite of what he had hoped.

It really doesn't make any sense for us to compare ourselves to other people. Whether it's financially, spiritually, emotionally, physically, or something else - we will never be on exactly the same level as anybody else. There will *always* be somebody thinner, richer, or smarter than we are, and likewise, there will always be somebody who's less attractive, less financially successful, or less educated. If we spend our time "tooting our own horn" to let others know how great we are, we're not impressing anyone - we're really quite annoying! And every time we compare ourselves to others and fall short, we're making a withdrawal from our "self-worth account." Sometimes a lack of self-worth can lead to indulgence in destructive habits as we try to find comfort, such as excessive eating or shopping, or even the abuse of drugs or alcohol. Ironically, the things we turn to for comfort actually damage us even more, especially if we develop an addiction. So, how do we stop ourselves from engaging in this unpleasant habit of comparing ourselves to others?

The Only Valid Comparisons are Those Within Ourselves

The only comparisons that truly count are the ones we make within ourselves. Consider the example of an acquaintance of mine who was tremendously overweight 20 years ago. Ten years ago he finally realized that he had to do something. He gradually began to cut back on the amounts he ate and he started to exercise a little bit. Today, he exercises six times a week and is in the best shape of his life. When he says, "I'm in better shape now than I was 20 years ago," he's not bragging – he's making a factual statement. He's not putting anyone else down; he's making a comparison *within himself* – a comparison of where he used to be, and where he is right now. It's okay for him to pat himself on the back. In fact, we *need* to give ourselves that occasional "I'm doing something right!" affirmation. Part of loving ourselves is seeing where we've made improvements and congratulating ourselves for having made them. To recognize progress in ourselves is not being prideful – it's not thinking, "I'm better than everybody else." It's important to acknowledge the things we have done right, the improvements we have made. Unless we do this from time to time, we'll end up feeling like a car that's run out of fuel.

> **Part of loving ourselves is seeing where we've made improvements and congratulating ourselves for having made them.**

Don't compare where you are now to where you someday hope to be. Compare where you are now to where you were a few days ago. Then you'll get dozens of bite-sized chunks of fulfillment – and a never-ending supply of things to be thankful for."[1]

This is an internal dialogue, not something we announce publicly. But doing so motivates us to keep moving in the right direction.

What are your priorities?

If we make a comparison within ourselves and discover that we're going downhill in some regard, then we need to decide whether the strength or skill we're losing is still a priority for us. If it's *not* a priority any longer, then it's time to stop feeling guilty and move on! If it *is* still a priority, then we need to decide *what* we will do about it. What action do we need to take?

For example, I have a friend who was a great tennis player 15 years ago. He exercised frequently and was in very good physical condition. About 10 years ago, however, he started cutting back on his exercise. There was a lot of stress in his life, and five years ago, he stopped playing tennis completely. Last year, he started to have health problems. Now he's taking medication, is in pain all the time, has gained an extra 50 pounds, and is not taking care of himself. It's time for some self-assessment! If he were to compare his current situation with his condition 15 years ago, he would undoubtedly realize that he's not doing as well now as he was then. Perhaps his thought process would go something like,

"Fifteen years ago I was doing great, 10 years ago I was not so bad, five years ago I was starting to slip, but now I've really gone downhill."

Hopefully his next thought would be, "It's time to take action!" If he doesn't make some changes, the quality of his life will continue to be negatively affected. And as he decides what action to take, there's another question he needs to ask himself: is being a great tennis player *still a priority* for him? At his age, most likely his priority should be to enjoy good health, not to become a tennis pro.

It's also important to ask ourselves the *right* questions when we evaluate our priorities. Many women I've worked with beat themselves up about their weight, especially as they get older. Of course their bodies aren't going to be the same as when they were 18! But instead of asking themselves if it's still a priority to be a perfect "10," the question they ask should be, "Is it a priority for me to be healthy?" The assumption is that most of us would answer that question in the affirmative. So the next question to ask oneself would be, "What does healthy look and feel like for someone like me?" (Factors such as age, overall health and body-type should be taken into consideration.)

Periodic Self-Assessment Is Important

Our priorities can change for lots of reasons, not just because of aging. A few years ago, a woman asked me to counsel her 17-year-old son, who was depressed. He was a senior in high school, had been accepted by the college he wanted to attend, was the quarterback of the football team, a straight-A student, good looking, and had a great family, yet he was depressed. His parents didn't know what to do. From the age of 6 until he was 14, he had played the piano and he had tremendous talent. Everybody thought he'd become a concert pianist. He practiced two hours every day! But at age 14, a change occurred. He found something new: football. He became proficient at playing football and earned the position of starting quarterback for the high school team. He completely gave up piano and focused his energy on football. People still frequently asked him to play the piano for them, but he hadn't been practicing, so he would decline. I realized that he was comparing the way he played at 17, when he no longer practiced, to the way he used to play when he was 14. He was beating himself up because he didn't play the piano as well anymore.

> "Ryan [not his real name]," I asked him, "What are your priorities right now?"
>
> His response was, "To play football, go to college, and get my degree." Not once did he mention playing the piano.
>
> "Is being a concert pianist still a priority for you in your life?" I asked.
>
> He immediately and quite emphatically replied, "No way!"
>
> 'Then why are you beating yourself up over it?"
>
> "I don't really know."

I told him he had the right to change his focus, and asked whether he thought it was time to let go of the piano priority. He had already let go of it physically when he started playing football instead of practicing his music, but he hadn't let go of it mentally. This resulted in an inner conflict, so he never played. I pointed out that he could still play piano recreationally and entertain himself, his friends and family. He was still a very capable player, but he needed to let go of the pressure of feeling that piano was his number one priority. Once Ryan realized being a concert pianist was not his heart's desire, the stress he had put upon himself evaporated. His mom called me a few days later and asked, "What did you do? He's his old happy self again!"

Ryan went off to college and continues to do well. His parents had been considering putting him on medication because he seemed so depressed. Yet all it took for him to be happy was to understand his true priorities.

Positive Leading Questions

As we engage in self-assessment from time-to-time, we need to be cautious about the approach we take. It's easy to ask the wrong questions and end up mired in self-criticism, which is discouraging and can keep us from making positive changes. There aren't many things that are more demotivating than getting down on ourselves. More importantly, criticizing ourselves is not conducive to loving ourselves.

So as we evaluate our priorities and our current situation, we need to ask ourselves positive leading questions. If we ask, "What's wrong with me?" guess what? The computer that's called our brain will give us a printout of all the things that are wrong with us; a laundry list of all the things we've done, said or thought that are wrong! The same principle applies to asking, "what's wrong with my wife/husband," or "what's wrong with my kids?" Instead, change the questions to, "What's RIGHT with my life?" 'What's RIGHT with my wife/husband?" and "What's RIGHT with my kids?" If we ask positive leading questions, we will get positive answers. Sadly, most of us are in the habit of asking ourselves questions that will have a negative outcome. As you change your focus to asking positive questions, be patient. If you're not used to looking for positive answers, they may not come quickly at first.

When we receive a positive answer, the brain responds by sending out endorphins, which create a state of happiness. This also applies to asking, "What do I like about *myself?*" Many people have never even considered asking themselves that question. But it's an important part of recognizing our own self-worth, our value as people.

As unique human beings, I believe each one of us is of infinite worth. Somehow along the way, most of us have lost that vision or understanding of our value. It's easier to see it in a newborn baby than in a troubled or moody teenager. Somewhere along the way, oftentimes starting at home and then at school, the negative withdrawals take their toll on us. The end result is that our self-worth suffers.

If it is a Priority, Take Action!

> *Where there is no vision, the people perish.*
> **— Proverbs 29:18**

Once you've decided something is a priority, what will you do about it? Taking action successfully requires the creation of a plan. But how often do we set goals, only to realize a few weeks later they have "gone by the wayside?" For example, almost everybody makes New Year's resolutions. Unfortunately, by February 1st, many of these resolutions have been retired. It is human nature to become enthusiastic and make promises to ourselves, but excitement and the adrenaline of "newness" can only motivate us for a short while. Part of the problem is that many of our goals tend to be rather generic, such as: "I'd like to get in better shape…" or "I'd like to be a better parent to my kids." As Jerry Seinfeld would say, "not that there's anything wrong with it. . ." but these types of goals are so vague, it is hard to know if any progress has been achieved.

Making S.M.A.R.T. Goals

> *Goals you don't pursue aren't goals, they're dreams, and dreams only make you happy when you're dreaming.*
> —Jeff Haden

For us to be successful beyond setting goals – i.e., so that we actually take the steps necessary to achieve them - we need to do two things: the first is to make what are called "SMART" goals: **S**pecific, **M**easurable, **A**ttainable, **R**elevant and **T**ime-bound. The second is to be held accountable. As an example, S.M.A.R.T. goals for getting in shape or losing some weight could look like the following:

1. I will lift weights every other day and do 30 minutes of cardio (walking, running, and treadmill) on the intervening days.
2. I will consult with a nutritionist within the next 2 weeks to create a healthy and balanced diet.
3. I will implement this new daily nutritional regimen, and therefore create a new and healthier lifestyle.

4. I will lose 15 pounds within the next five months and therefore reach my ideal weight.

Be Held Accountable

Setting S.M.A.R.T. goals by themselves is not a guarantee for success. We also need to be accountable to someone. For those of us who are very disciplined, this may seem a little unnecessary, but experience proves otherwise for the majority of us. Pick your best friend, a co-worker, your spouse or a coach. Having someone to answer to greatly increases the probability of our getting things done. Besides accountability, it's also good to have someone encouraging us as we try to reach our goals.

The Inner Critic

There's a phenomenon I've seen with many of my clients that I call "the inner critic." Once I get to know a client, it becomes fairly clear whether they have an inner critic, because those who do are very hard on themselves. The inner critic takes over people's lives gradually, eventually becoming the pervasive voice in their minds. I liken it to God handing a person the keys to their destiny in the form of a car: they start out driving their new car, but then the inner critic speaks up, and they move into the passenger seat. The inner critic begins to take over, and the driver moves to the back seat. Finally, the inner critic becomes so powerful, the driver ends up in the trunk where they have no influence over where the car is going! Yet it's *their car!!* If a person is mired in self-criticism, they have no control over their destiny. The goal for such people is to reclaim their lives after the inner critic has taken control. Once a person is back in the "driver's seat," they may hear the inner critic say, "You're not good enough." But they can refuse to give it any credibility and respond, "I heard what you said, but I choose not to believe it!" It's putting the inner critic back in his place. For some of us, the inner critic never fully goes away. The key is to not let him take over your life, by refusing to believe him.

The Burden of Perfectionism

"My name is Elia, and I'm a recovering perfectionist!" There was a time early in my life when I wasn't comfortable with any of my imperfections. Like many other people, I didn't like to admit I had weaknesses. I had to pretend that I knew everything - that I was always right, and I tried to cover up my flaws. It was so much pressure! The need to be perfect, not to be able to admit mistakes, meant having to maintain a façade. That required *a lot of effort*! Not to mention that it was disingenuous, because it wasn't the *real* me.

Then I had an epiphany one day when **I realized that I would rather be happy, than be right.** Recognizing that I didn't have to be right all the time was the beginning of the disassembling of the perfectionist part of me. And what a relief that was! When we can admit we've hurt somebody's feelings, or can ask for forgiveness, it makes it so much easier for us to be our true selves. The more we own up to our imperfections, the easier it gets – and the *lighter* we become. We shed many "pounds" of emotional baggage, accumulated from trying so hard to maintain the perfect appearance.

Show me a person who's unhappy, and I'll show you a person who has a hard time accepting themselves and their imperfections. Human nature is such that we focus far more on our imperfections than on our accomplishments. If you want to be truly happy, and really love yourself, embrace yourself and accept that you're not perfect. Turn back to your true nature and stop trying to maintain a façade of perfection.

Be the Real You

> *What other people think –*
> *especially people you don't even know – doesn't matter.*
> *What other people want you to do doesn't matter.*
> —Jeff Haden

Somewhere early on in life, we pick up the baggage of believing we have to maintain an appearance to gain the approval of others. We act the way we think other people expect us to be, playing a role, hoping for acceptance. As this notion takes root in our subconscious, by the time we are college aged, we're leading a double life. The real person is hidden deeper and deeper within. Many of us go through life so fearful of appearing "uncool," imperfect, or foolish! We think the world wants us to be a certain way, so we try to live up to that. But why should we want to be like everybody else? When did *that* become part of the criteria for acceptance? There's a direct link between being true to yourself, and finding happiness. Otherwise, we go through life trying to be somebody else, and we battle our true nature. Personally, I don't want to play a *role* for the rest of my life - I want to be the *real* me! As Dr. Wayne Dyer has said, "What other people think of me is none of my business!"

Bonnie Ware worked in palliative care, spending time with patients who had only a few months to live. Their most common regret was, "I wish I'd had the courage to live a life true to myself, not the life others expected of me."[2]

Why Do We Play Roles?

Why do we play roles, hide our imperfections, and try to pretend to be somebody we're really not? There is a part of each of us that believes, "If they TRULY knew the real me, they'd reject me." It's human nature to feel that way.

I work with a lot of people who are very successful by the world's standards – presidents, executives or CEO's of thriving companies – who are so insecure, it's shocking. They don't love themselves. In the confidentiality of my office, people open up their hearts. Deep down inside, they're insecure little boys or girls. They don't believe that they deserve the success they've achieved, so they subconsciously try to cut themselves down to size.

Everybody feels like a fraud at some point – like "I don't know as much as people think I know, and somebody's going to figure that out." When we finally understand that it's okay not to know everything, it's very liberating. When you love yourself enough, it doesn't really matter what other people think. We don't *need* other people's approval to be who we are. It's nice to have others' approval and to have people say nice things about us – but it's not necessary for our own personal happiness.

Taking Care of Ourselves

Establishing our true priorities and being our true selves are not the only things we need to do to love ourselves. **We also need to take care of ourselves.**

Several months ago I ran into a long-time family friend. I was surprised by the way she looked, and commented, "You look great!" She replied by telling me that she had lost over 30 pounds! We chatted for a while, and then I asked her how she was able to keep all that weight off. She told me something that really made me stop and think. She said that she had made the decision not to eat anything unless it was "in her best interest!" A few weeks later we hosted her son's wedding reception at our house. It was a big feast with lots of food and even more dessert. Toward the end of the meal, I totally forgot about my friend's dieting routine. There was one huge piece of cake left and I offered it to her. With a smile, she politely declined by saying, "No thanks, it's not in my best interest!" I was struck again by how simple yet profound that statement was – the recognition that she had the freedom to say "no" to anything that was not good for her. To look at it another way, when a decision between a short-term temptation was at odds with her long-term welfare, she chose her long-term welfare. This principle is most commonly known as self-discipline, viewed through the consciousness of wanting to build a better future, one decision at a time. I like to call it "the NIMBI Principle" (Not In My Best Interest!) Any time we give in to self-destructive behavior, we are hurting ourselves. Since we all have areas where we need to improve, how can we best make use of this wonderful little phrase? When might this be applicable in your life?

Siblings, spouses, relatives, or other well-meaning people in our lives may sometimes offer enticements. For example, if you've been trying to quit smoking, a friend might offer you a cigarette, possibly not knowing you've committed to stop. From now on, whenever somebody asks you to do something you know deep down inside isn't in your best interest, remember the NIMBI Principle, and turn down the invitation.

What I love about this simple saying is how empowering it feels to say it. Could you say it without judgment, but with a smile, just like my friend?

> "More cake anyone?"
> " NIMBI!"
> "Want to smoke a cigarette?"
> "NIMBI! "
> "Want to stay up all night and party?"
> Again, "NIMBI!"

By choosing what's right for ourselves, we're taking care of ourselves. And that's an important part of loving ourselves. I hope we can make this part of our daily lexicon. It will bless our lives and maybe even give others permission to do the same. "It's not in my best interest!" What a lovely phrase!

Forgive Yourself

Since forgiveness is so vital to our overall state of happiness, this book has an entire chapter dedicated to the concept. The most important type of forgiveness is for us to forgive ourselves (see Chapter Six).

Chapter Four

The First Path: Love Yourself
Part 2 - Achieve Balance in Your Life

"Pan Metron Ariston!"

— Aristotle

As I mentioned before, I grew up in Greece. Over and over again in elementary school I heard the phrase "Pan metron ariston" – "all things in moderation" – because it was considered so important. The ancient Greeks led very well-balanced lives. That's what made them such a great civilization. They studied and progressed in multiple disciplines: the arts, mathematics, sciences, and athletics. The same principle of having balance that made Greek civilization so successful applies to us as individuals. We need balance in our lives – physical, emotional, intellectual, and spiritual. There was a time when my life was out of balance because I was working too many hours a day and mostly ignoring my needs for exercise, time with my family, and recreation. I got sick. And until I put things back in balance, I kept getting sicker.

PHYSICAL BALANCE

A lot of people struggle with achieving physical balance. Eating disorders and obesity are at an all-time high; addictions to drugs and alcohol have become epidemic. So many people are unable to achieve a restful night's sleep that sleep disorder clinics have sprung up all over the United States.

What are the criteria for having a physically balanced life? We need to maintain a healthy weight, exercise, eat well, and get enough sleep. If we don't manage those factors, *they* will manage *us*. In other words, we'll end up having a heart attack, stroke, diabetes, or some other health crisis.

When you took the life satisfaction survey in Chapter Two, how did you respond to statement #3, "My life is in balance physically" The options were "never," "rarely" "sometimes," "often," or "always." A response of "sometimes" is like a yellow traffic light. If your answer was "rarely" or "never," that's a definite red light! If your life is not physically in balance, it will affect *every aspect* of your life. You will have reduced productivity at work, you may be more unpleasant in your personal relationships, and you just won't feel good! Even a response of "sometimes" means it's time to take action. Maybe you should meet with a nutritionist, a personal trainer, or an expert in sleep disorders. Most people who take the survey tend to answer somewhere in the middle, but is life truly satisfying if one is physically in balance only "some of the time"? The answer is, "No!" People whose lives are out of balance physically are simply not very happy. There are a number of things we can do to help get our lives into good physical balance:

1. Maintain a healthy weight. We live in a society of disposable goods. When something gets old or worn out, we throw it away and replace it.

We can't do that with our bodies. This is it – we only get one, and we need to take care of it. We also tend to live in crisis management mode most of the time. We wait to make changes until a doctor tells us we're going to have a heart attack if we don't make a change. Sometimes we even wait until *after* the heart attack happens before we finally take action, and that is always more expensive financially, more draining emotionally, and more taxing physically. We need to become more proactive! Prevention is *far* less expensive than crisis management, and also far less traumatic. If I change the oil in my car every 3,000 miles, I spend $30 every time I do it. But if I don't change the oil, the engine burns up and that's way more expensive. The same principle applies to our bodies. It's much harder to lose weight at 300 pounds than it is to stop gaining weight at 160 pounds and realize we need to lose 10 pounds.

Obesity affects every aspect of a person's life. I had a client once, an empty nester who was in her late 50's, who had been overweight since she was a teenager. Food was her solace. If she was angry, she ate. If she was sad, she ate. The refrigerator was her best friend. She got heavier and heavier, and became more and more unhappy, until finally, she decided to undergo gastric bypass surgery. It's a fairly drastic operation, and it put a lot of strain on her heart. Her doctor told her that she should never go through it again. And although she did lose weight, she was concerned that she would go back to her old ways and re-gain it all. Her response to stress continued to be eating. Finally one day she said to me, "I'm afraid if I continue this way and need another surgery, it will kill me! What can I do, so I never go back to my old habits?" I suggested she post the following two questions on her refrigerator door so she would see them each time she felt like eating:

"Am I hungry physically?

Or am I hungry emotionally?"

So she put a sign on the refrigerator door where she couldn't help but see it. I told her that when she was physically hungry she should open the refrigerator and eat a healthy snack. If she were emotionally hungry she should journal her feelings, or pick up the phone and talk to a trusted friend. She took the advice, and as a result, she has been able to maintain a healthy weight for the first time in 50 years.

Many of us need to reevaluate our relationship to food. If we answer those two questions every time we go to the refrigerator or the pantry, we may find ourselves eating less frequently. If we're hungry physically, then by all means we should eat a healthy snack. If we're hungry emotionally (for example, because of an upsetting phone call), then we need to deal with whatever upset us. We have the choice, right at that point, to deal with whatever came up, or to postpone dealing with it by eating, thereby creating another problem in our lives: damaging our physical health.

Since we can't just *stuff* those feelings down our throat with food, what can we do? There are at least three ways we can respond when we're emotionally hungry:

1. A great step is to get on an exercise bike, go for a fast walk, or do something else physical to process that energy.
2. If physical activity isn't possible, we can write things down, journal our feelings, and describe exactly how we feel; or
3. We can pick up the phone and connect with another human being: a trusted friend, relative, or adviser.

We can then vent and process those feelings. Afterward, the desire to eat will have diminished.

We should all have a concrete goal when it comes to maintaining a healthy weight. Determine what your ideal weight is, if necessary, with the help of your doctor, and work to get there or to maintain it if you're already there. Those of us who want to lose weight may want the assistance of a reputable weight loss program.

For some people, weight loss is simply a matter of changing to a healthier diet. If you need to reevaluate the way you eat, see a nutritionist. For others, it's a matter of portion control. We should never eat anything bigger than the size of our fist. If we do that 4-6 times a day, we should be just fine.

2. Exercise. Everybody needs to exercise to feel good, regardless of whether they need to lose weight. This is not about becoming a tri-athlete. It's more about getting your heart pumping. A good exercise program usually includes cardiovascular exercises for 30 minutes, every day. It's not necessary that you join a gym or spend money having an elaborate workout program designed. Going for a daily walk costs nothing, but the results will be wonderful. It may help to get an exercise buddy. Working out with a friend can really help us to stay motivated and get us out of the house. The important point is to start *before* you get to some kind of health crisis. Your age doesn't matter, either. It's never too late to reap the benefits of exercise.

3. Eat Right. In his book *Good Stress: Living Younger, Longer*, Dr. Terry Lyles discusses the importance of optimal nutritional health:

"Our society has programmed us to follow eating habits that impede optimal health. How many meals do you think you should eat every day? Two? Three? Four or more? If you're like most people, you probably answered three, because that is what our society has taught us. But that is wrong.

What if I told you that we should eat five or six times a day? That really is how we should eat for optimal nutritional health. Why? Because eating five or six times a day (or approximately every three hours) coincides with our body's cycle for regulating blood sugar level. Glycemic levels oscillate in three-hour cycles, so food consumption should be compatible with this. Our long digestive tract is better designed to handle five or six small meals and snacks throughout the day rather than two or three large meals consumed at longer intervals . . .

* * *

The ideal arrangement would be three small meals a day interspersed with three light snacks.

* * *

Eating lighter and more often helps us be light and lean and full of energy throughout the day. It keeps our metabolism burning faster, even when we are asleep. Our metabolism naturally slows down as we age but eating smaller portions more frequently will speed it up again. And speeding up our metabolism burns fat."[1]

My health suffered the most when I wasn't following Dr. Lyles' advice. I frequently skipped breakfast (the most important meal of the day), grabbed a quick bite from some fast food place for lunch on the run, and finally, exhausted and starving, I'd eat a big, heavy dinner at night, then fall into bed. That was a recipe for disaster and I paid a big price for it, health-wise.

4. Rest Occasionally and Get Enough Sleep. As we rush around our busy days, it's very easy to forget to stop and "catch our breath" once in a while. When we don't, we become completely worn out, as well as less productive. In *Good Stress: Living Younger, Longer,* Dr. Lyles explains that

> "Our bodies require brief recovery periods every 90-120 minutes throughout the day. This is in addition to the 6-8 hours of high quality recovery sleep we need every night to replenish our energy reserves . . .
>
> A daily recovery strategy does not need to be complicated or time- consuming: we're talking about a 2-5 minute recovery break after every 90-120 minutes of work."[2]
>
> "Our bodies . . . have a small energy fuel tank. Its energy capacity can carry us at peak performance for 90-120 minutes before we need a "pit stop" to refuel and recharge. After two hours, our performance begins to drop off drastically. So we need a 2-5 minute pit stop to energize us fully for the next 90-120 minute rotation. Believe me, if you implement this simple technique of building regular rest/recovery periods in your day, you will notice a difference in your performance within the first week."[3]

People who feel sleepy in the middle of the day should take a nap or rest when they have the opportunity and not feel guilty about it. It is part of the natural sleep cycle that we feel less alert mid-day. This can be intensified by a big meal, such as a business lunch. While our culture in the United States doesn't seem to take this into consideration, many Latin American and tropical countries recognize this need and have daily siesta time in the early afternoon. If we fulfill our need to take an occasional 20 minute nap, we'll be much more productive, more efficient, and actually end up getting more done. And we'll feel better on top of it!

As Dr. Lyles stated in his book, we also need to get a full night's sleep. When we don't get enough sleep, we tend to be irritable, moody, easily moved to tears, and impatient. We can't and won't function to the best of our ability. And there are more serious ramifications of being sleep-deprived, beyond just affecting our moods and performance:

> "Sleep deprivation can, in fact, undermine all areas of your physical and mental health. Sleep deprivation weakens the immune system leaving us more susceptible to other diseases and disorders like diabetes, cancer and even the common cold. It is not uncommon for people who suffer from sleep deprivation due to sleep disorders - sleep apnea, narcolepsy, insomnia, etc. - to also suffer from other problems including diabetes, asthma or a second sleep disorder."[4]

A step toward better physical balance is to make a commitment to yourself: plan a reasonable time by which you will be in bed every night, and stick to it. Try to get up at the same time every morning. And if you find yourself winding down during the middle of the day and it's possible to take a 20-minute nap, do it! You'll be on your way to a healthier, happier lifestyle.

EMOTIONAL BALANCE

Emotionally balanced people are content with themselves, at peace, and happy. But how often do we reflect upon whether we're emotionally balanced? How many of us, when we make our New Year's Resolutions decide, "I'm going to get into emotional balance"? It's much more common to think about improving our physical balance. Emotional balance is just as important to being happy, however, and there are steps that can be taken to achieve it:

1. Make Time for Yourself. Often as adults we forget that we have our own individual needs. Work, children, elderly parents, or our busy lives can keep us running so fast that it's easy to forget about ourselves. Then we wake up one day and realize we no longer recognize ourselves. We all need to make time for ourselves. Think about taking a class or doing some other activity one night a week – something you enjoy. If you need "down time," then close the door, burn candles, take a bubble bath, or put on pajamas and get in bed with a good book. If you have children, your spouse will need to coordinate with you and help out with this. If you're a single parent, one option is to find another single parent with whom you can trade off. They undoubtedly are in just as much need of a little "R & R" as you.

Particularly in the case of women, being a little bit "selfish" is a good thing. When I tell a female client to be a little more "selfish," I have to explain that I don't mean she should become more self-centered; it's about self-preservation. There's a difference. I've had the same conversation with many women, and it's almost like a foreign concept to them, as if they believe there's something wrong with saying "no" to taking on another project, or something wrong with taking time for themselves. But both are absolutely essential to having emotional balance. The "time-out" can be extravagant, like a weeklong trip to a spa, or as simple as going to lunch with a girlfriend. Regardless, it's important to take a break from the normal stresses of life. Women know all too well that their jobs never end!

2. Reduce the noise! Our modern world just seems to keep getting faster and louder. Due to advancements in technology such as computers, the Internet, tablets, and cell phones, life moves at lightning speed. People are being overwhelmed by the noise of our electronic world, and may not even realize it. There's so much noise! Have you ever tried going without electronics for a week? How about for three days? For 24 hours? If you haven't, you should try it. Turn off your iPod®, tablet, your TV, and your phones. You'll be amazed at how different things feel when you're not being constantly bombarded by electronic stimulation. Shawn Moon's book *On Your Own*[5] describes a challenge given to a group of "twenty-somethings" by an ecclesiastical leader. He called it a "media fast," and the experiment was for those young adults to spend 30 days without any media in any form: no music, movies, video games, television, or internet. At first, those who took on the challenge found it to be tough. It didn't take long for them to realize how pervasive and addictive those pursuits were. They suffered from "withdrawal," and said they struggled to find things to do. After a few days, however, it got easier to avoid all forms of media, and they gradually lost their desire for them. They spent more time with friends, read more, and spent more time actually talking with other people.

While you probably don't want to cut yourself off from all media, you can create a calmer environment for yourself by **limiting the amount of time you engage with it.** For example, you can resist the urge to check your email every 10 minutes, stop racing to answer a text every time one comes in, and try limiting the number of hours the television and radio are blaring away in your home. Instead of being a slave to media, let it enhance your life – when you have the time for it.

3. Engage in Social Interaction. As human beings, we need face-to-face social interaction. We're not an island – we're not meant to be isolated. It's sad to note that when somebody goes on a shooting rampage, they're frequently described by their neighbors as "loners." I've often wondered if the shooter had had more social interaction with friends and neighbors whether the tragedy could have been avoided.

Social interaction does not mean social networking. There is a difference. I love Facebook and the old acquaintances with whom I've been able to reconnect because of it. But it's not the kind of face-to-face social interaction we need as human beings.

You may need to *plan* for social interaction in your life. If you don't get much because you work from home or you are a stay-at-home parent, it might help to schedule a weekly social activity such as a group lunch, a "ladies/guy's night out," or participate in a book club.

4. Manage Stress. How often do you run into somebody, ask how they are, and hear the answer, "Oh, I'm all stressed out!" That has become so commonplace in our society, it's almost synonymous with "good morning." Imagine instead the following conversation:

> "How are you today?"
> "I'm doing great! I have zero stress in my life!"

It sounds almost bizarre, it's so foreign! We live in a fast-paced world with increasing demands for our time and resources and it seems like we're a nation, if not a world, of stressed-out people. Why has stress become such a daily part of our lives, and what can we do about it? Is stress always a bad thing? It certainly has a negative connotation.

I can't foresee a time in the future when stress will be eliminated from the world. We all have stress at work, at home (many families struggle with issues like finances or unemployment), and sometimes in our relationships. When we experience too much stress in our lives, the result can be health issues, irritability, sleep disturbance, depression, and other unpleasant side effects. We can no longer give our best selves to our relationships. At some point, we need to realize, "This isn't working. What can I do?" There are three possible choices:

1. We can continue to try to live with stress, which doesn't work. It's not sustainable, because it increasingly affects every aspect of your life in a negative way.
2. We can try to eliminate stress completely, which is not realistic; or
3. We can manage stress and learn from it, which is the best option.

Rather than having stress *run* our lives, why don't we use stress as a catalyst to *improve* our lives? A great example is my friend who taught me about the NIMBI Principle. She was feeling tremendous stress because of her weight. She could have let it steamroll her. Instead, she used it as an incentive to recognize that her eating habits at the time weren't doing her any favors.

Following are a number of strategies we can use to manage stress:

a) Operate in Prevention Mode. Part of the problem we face in trying to handle stress is that most of us are constantly operating in crisis-management mode rather than taking a proactive approach to our lives. We have to continually put out fires, going from one thing to the next. Can you visualize yourself going through life carrying a fire extinguisher all the time? Putting out fires to the left, to the right, above and below you? That's no way to live! Living in a reactive mode will never bring peace of mind or happiness.

> **Living in a reactive mode will never bring peace of mind or happiness.**

> *Maintaining order rather than correcting disorder is the ultimate principle of wisdom. To cure disease after it has appeared is like digging a well when one feels thirsty, or forging weapons after the war has already begun.*
> —**Nei Jing, 2nd century BC**

Crisis *prevention* is the key because it's less expensive financially, physically, emotionally and mentally than crisis *management*. This is true with regard to every aspect of our lives. Wouldn't it be better for us to change some habits now, like eating healthier and exercising, rather than waiting for a crisis, such as a heart attack, to hit and force us to make those changes? Wouldn't it be more prudent to address our marital issues now, rather than waiting until the divorce papers show up? What about learning to live within our means with an actual budget, rather than accumulating debt, which could lead us to bankruptcy?

It's also important to say "no" once in a while. Doing so doesn't make one a bad person. If we can never say "no," we end up taking on too much. And there's *always* a price to pay when we do that.

Consider all the unnecessary emotional and mental stress we're putting ourselves through by not acting on our issues *before* they get out of control. Most things in life can be prevented if we take the time to address them.

b) Take Time to Assess. Basically, **mismanagement of stress is a long-term neglect of our needs**. Long-term exposure to stress can make us physically sick or lead to emotional and mental breakdowns. How do we change our mindset from dealing with crises all the time to taking charge of our lives? We need to stop, ponder and meditate on the direction of our work, our family, and every other aspect of our lives. It's a key ingredient to successfully managing our overall stress levels.

I've had quite a few clients who are business executives working way too many hours. They don't take time for themselves. They become so overwhelmed, their lifestyle is more reactive crisis management than crisis prevention. When doing executive coaching, I frequently have to ask,

> "When was the last time you actually took a day off to contemplate, to think about the direction of your life? Or two days off? Time to do something others might think

of as nonproductive? When you didn't make appointments, go to meetings, close any deals, answer any phone calls, or return any emails? Instead, you sat, pondered, and meditated about the direction of your life, the direction of your company, or the direction of your family?"

The typical pushback is, "I can't afford to take a day off!"

And my immediate response is, "You can't afford NOT to take a day off!"

It is the same for the rest of us. To effectively manage our stress, we need to occasionally ponder the direction our lives are taking. The result might be that you'll make a necessary course correction. This may not only add quality years to your life, but it will also add balance and perspective. As a result, you'll be a better spouse, employee, parent, friend and, ultimately, a better person. Your most vital relationships will get the benefit of the best you, including your relationship with yourself. It's important to occasionally take a life time-out, even for a day, and see the benefits of learning to manage your stress better, rather than allowing stress to manage you.

c) Set Limits on Yourself. Setting limits can help to eliminate some of the stressors in our lives. For example, if you're struggling with over-commitment, part of learning to set limits is having the ability to say "no" and not feel guilty about it. When I was younger, I didn't have the ability to say "no" because I was a people-pleaser. As I have gotten older, saying "no" has become a lot easier for me.

Given the increased demands on my time, I've learned to say "no" and it's actually a way of taking care of myself. Over-commitment increases our stress levels, and our relationships, our health and our productivity will suffer. We then feel overwhelmed, and our stress level increases even more.

Setting limits on our activities is a part of self-preservation. It's so easy to run ourselves ragged! Much like a racecar, we can't operate at full speed indefinitely, because we'll blow a gasket. Either something will crack physically, or we'll be mentally or emotionally drained. A nervous breakdown is a long time coming. It results from long-term exposure to a high amount of stress.

d) Parent Yourself! What we really need to do is parent ourselves. Most parents don't neglect their kids - they're very mindful of their needs, especially when they're young. They feed them, clothe them, bathe them, love them, and get them to bed at a reasonable hour. But how many of us are good at parenting ourselves?

When working with clients who are neglecting themselves, I've found it's very effective to compare the way they treat themselves to the way they take care of their children. For example, if a person is so busy that they forget to eat, I'll ask them, "Can you imagine not feeding your child breakfast and lunch tomorrow?" Of course, they're always shocked at the prospect, but then I point out that that's what they're doing to themselves!

If I ask them why they take care of their children, the response is always, "I *have* to! If I don't, then who will?" I then point out that the same principle applies to us as adults: **if we don't take care of ourselves, who will?**

Sometimes we're so busy we deprive ourselves of the most fundamental things: sleep and food. Can you imagine having the following conversation with your child?

> "You need to stay on the computer until 2:00 a.m. to keep checking your email!
> "But Mom/Dad, I'm tired, I want to go to sleep!"
> "NO! Go back to the computer and check to see if you have any new emails!"

How often do we say *to ourselves*, "Go to bed! You need your sleep"? We frequently say it to our children; to ourselves, we don't say it very often.

If a client is putting harmful substances in their body, I ask them if they would give it to their child. The thought of doing so is shocking to them. But why is it so easy for us to take care of our kids, but not take care of ourselves? I believe it's because we lack adequate self-parenting.

> **I believe it's because we lack adequate self-parenting.**

SPIRITUAL BALANCE

Several years ago I encountered a phrase written by Pierre Teilhard de Chardin: **"We're not physical beings having a spiritual experience; we're spiritual beings having a physical experience."** It completely changed my paradigm. Having spiritual balance in our lives is such an important part of personal happiness that there's an entire chapter devoted to it in this book: "The Fifth Path: Nourishing Your Spirit."

INTELLECTUAL DEVELOPMENT

Another important aspect of personal happiness is developing intellectually, which is discussed in greater detail in Chapter Seven, "The Fourth Path: Following Your Passion."

My personal experience has been that when I'm in the process of learning something new and expanding my horizons, I tend to feel much more alive, and as a result, happier.

You yourself, as much as anybody in the entire universe, deserve your love and affection.
—**Buddha**

Chapter Four: The First Path: Love Yourself (Part 2) **81**

Points to Ponder:
1. Consider how to incorporate the NIMBI principle into your life.
2. A balanced life is a happy life.
3. Perfectionism is not your friend.

Questions to Consider:
1. Do you compare yourself to others?
2. Do you "parent" yourself?
3. Is your life physically, emotionally and spiritually balanced?

Note to the Reader: This chapter has more Action steps than does any other chapter in this book, because loving yourself is so vital to overall happiness. Before moving on to the next chapter, you may want to devote two or three weeks (or longer, if necessary) to incorporating into your life the SMART goals (Specific, Measurable, Attainable, Relevant and Time-bound) you make when completing the following Action Steps.

Take Action

1. **Self-Assessment:** (Don't forget to ask Positive Leading Questions!)
What are the top priorities in your life? _____
_____
_____

Which of those priorities are you achieving? _____
_____

Which priorities, if any, are you not achieving? _____
_____

Are they still priorities? _____
Write SMART goals for each priority you are not achieving. _____
_____
_____

Write the name of the person you will ask to help you be accountable for achieving those goals: _____

Think about one aspect of each of the following areas of your life, and compare yourself to where you were 20, 10 and 5 years ago, last year, and now.

2. Physical Balance: (Examples: are you taking care of yourself? Are you maintaining a healthy weight, exercising, eating right, and getting enough sleep? This is so important, you should do this exercise for each one of those factors.)

20 years ago: _____

_____

_____

10 years ago: _____

_____

_____

5 years ago: _____

_____

_____

Last year: _____

_____

_____

Now: _____

_____

_____

Assessment: Have you improved? If so, congratulate yourself and give yourself a tangible reward!

Is there room for improvement? Consider whether the areas where you have slipped are still a priority.

What would you like to see happen over the next year? _____

_____

_____

Make an action plan using SMART goals and write it down here: _____

_____

3. **Emotional Balance:** (Examples: Do you make time for yourself? Are you overwhelmed by all the electronic noise in your life, or do you feel the amount in which you engage is appropriate? Do you have social interaction regularly? Is your stress level manageable?)

20 years ago: _____

_____

_____

10 years ago: _____

_____

_____

5 years ago: _____

_____

_____

Last year: _____

_____

_____

Now: _____

_____

_____

Assessment: Have you improved? If so, congratulate yourself and give yourself a tangible reward!

Is there room for improvement? Consider whether the areas where you have slipped are still a priority.

What would you like to see happen over the next year? _____

_____

Make an action plan using SMART goals and write it down here: _____

_____

_____

Chapter Five

The Second Path: Be Grateful

"Oh Lord, that lends me life, lend me a heart replete with thankfulness."
—*William Shakespeare*

STARTING THE PROCESS OF BECOMING HAPPIER IS REALLY QUITE EASY – it's all about changing our mood. And how do we change our mood? Typically, when people feel down it's because they're dwelling on what they wish they had, or what they used to have. It's the exact opposite of being grateful for what they *do* have. The quickest way to turn sadness on its head and become happier is in one key question we ask ourselves: "What am I grateful for?" **There's no way we can be sad if we're basking in gratitude.**

Many years ago, as young newlyweds, my wife Sona and I encountered a lady I'll never forget. Even though our interaction lasted only a few minutes, she had a tremendous impact on me. As I spotted her across the room, I thought that she must have been at least 120 years old! I have never seen more wrinkles on a human face, yet she had the most beautiful countenance, with piercing, sparkling blue eyes and snow-white hair. There was clearly something very special about her. Sona and I both wanted to meet her, so we walked over and introduced ourselves.

As she briefly told us about her life story, we learned that she grew up in rural Idaho, in a house that didn't even have indoor plumbing. Married for 40 years, she had 6 children, and spent most of her life working very, very hard on a farm. This lady was no stranger to heartache - she had lost one of her children at a young age, and had been widowed for 40 years. Yet she was stunningly beautiful because she was so full of love, and so full of light. Her beauty emanated from what was on the inside.

At her advanced age, she was so obviously happy after a difficult life, I wanted to know how she had done it. She smiled and responded, "That's easy! All you need is to have an *attitude of gratitude!*"

There was that phrase again . . . I had heard it so many times before, but this time it was different. I heard *this* woman say it with such conviction that it made an immediate and long-lasting impact. She personified it unlike anyone I had ever met before: despite her many hardships, she was grateful. She had lived this truth her entire life, and her entire being reflected it – especially her face. Wouldn't it be great to have lived a long and fruitful life and be *so* close to the end of one's mortal existence and still exude such happiness? That's success!

It's All About Perspective

The following story is a great illustration of how our perspective affects the way we view life:

How Poor Are We?

One day, the father of a very wealthy family took his son on a trip to the country with the purpose of showing him how poor people live. They spent a couple of days and nights on the farm of what would be considered a very poor family. On their return from their trip, the father asked his son, 'How was the trip?'

"It was great, Dad."

"Did you see how poor people live?" the father asked.

"Oh yeah," said the son.

"So, tell me, what did you learn from the trip?" asked the father

The son answered: "I saw that we have one dog and they had four.

We have a pool that reaches to the middle of our garden and they have a creek that has no end.

We have imported lanterns in our garden and they have the stars at night.

Our patio reaches to the front yard and they have the whole horizon.

We have a small piece of land to live on and they have fields that go beyond our sight.

We have servants who serve us, but they serve others.

We buy our food, but they grow theirs.

We have walls around our property to protect us, they have friends to protect them."

The boy's father was speechless. Then his son added, "Thanks Dad for showing me how poor we are."

—Author unknown

Perspective is a great thing. It makes one wonder what would happen if we all gave thanks for everything we have, instead of worrying about what we don't have. The following poem sums up the value of a grateful perspective pretty well:

> I AM THANKFUL for the wife who says it's hot dogs tonight, because she is home with me and not out with someone else.
>
> … for the husband who is on the sofa being a couch potato, because he is home with me and not out at the bars.
>
> … for the teenager who is complaining about doing the dishes because that means she is at home and not on the streets.
>
> … for the taxes that I pay because it means that I am employed.
>
> … for the mess to clean after a party because it means that I have been surrounded by friends.
>
> … for the clothes that fit a little too snug because it means I have enough to eat.
>
> … for my shadow that watches me work because it means I am out in the sunshine.

Chapter Five: The Second Path: Be Grateful

… for a lawn that needs mowing, windows that need cleaning, and gutters that need fixing, because it means I have a home.

… for all the complaining I hear about the government because it means that we have freedom of speech.

… for the parking spot I find at the far end of the parking lot because it means I am capable of walking and that I have been blessed with transportation.

… for my huge heating bill because it means I am warm.

… for the lady behind me in church that sings off-key because it means I can hear.

… for the pile of laundry and ironing because it means I have clothes to wear.

… for weariness and aching muscles at the end of the day because it means I have been capable of working hard.

… for the alarm that goes off in the early morning hours because it means that I am alive.

—Author unknown.

Adjusting our perspective to one of gratitude can truly change the way we see life. A great tool for becoming more grateful is to write down three things for which we are grateful, in the morning, every day, as soon as we get up. I do this myself, and the result is that my feelings of gratitude are without end.

In her book *The Hiding Place*,[1] Corrie Ten Boom recounted her experiences during the Holocaust of World War II. She spent some time as an inmate of the infamous Ravensbruck concentration camp. The living conditions were completely miserable, and the prisoners had only flea-infested straw mattresses upon which to sleep. At first, Corrie and her sister felt like the fleas were just another affliction to endure in the horrific conditions. But Corrie soon realized that the fleas were actually a blessing: the Nazi guards, who frequently beat and assaulted the prisoners, did not enter the barracks because they did not want to risk being infested with fleas.

Gratitude will bring us out of our "scarcity mentality" and into an "abundance mentality." A scarcity mentality means, "I never have enough," while an abundance mentality means "I have enough." Enough of whatever you need – whether it is stuff, love, time, friends, opportunities, or dreams.

On his website www.joelosteen.com, best-selling author and megachurch pastor Joel Osteen commented about how our minds will naturally gravitate toward the negative:

> "A study showed how positive and negative memories are handled by different parts of the brain. A negative memory takes up more space. There's more to process. Because of this, we remember the negative more than the positive. For example, a person will remember losing $50 more than they will remember gaining $50.[2]

If we maintain an attitude of gratitude, we will dwell on our positive memories. There just won't be time for negative thinking.

> *Find a place inside where there's joy, and the joy will burn out the pain.*
> —**Joseph Campbell**

Controlling Our Thoughts

Life is a grindstone. Whether it grinds us down or polishes us up depends on us!
— **Thomas L. Holdcroft**

We have the power to choose our thoughts. We can elect to dwell on the negative, the hurts and the pain we've experienced in life, or we can choose to let go of the things that drag us down, and focus on the positive aspects of our lives. Elizabeth Gilbert talked about this concept in her book *Eat, Pray, Love:*

> . . . I can choose my thoughts.
>
> This last concept is a radically new idea for me. Richard from Texas brought it to my attention recently, when I was complaining about my inability to stop brooding. He said, ". . . you need to learn how to select your thoughts just the same way you select what clothes you're gonna wear every day. This is a power you can cultivate. If you want to control things in your life so bad, work on the mind. That's the only thing you should be trying to control.
>
> On first glance, this seems a nearly impossible task. Control your *thoughts?* Instead of the other way around? . . .
>
> I've started being vigilant about watching my thoughts all day, and monitoring them. I repeat this vow about 700 times a day: "I will not harbor unhealthy thoughts anymore." Every time a diminishing thought arises, I repeat the vow. *I will not harbor unhealthy thoughts anymore.* The first

> time I heard myself say this, my inner ear perked up at the word "harbor," which is a noun as well as a verb. A harbor, of course, is a place of refuge, a port of entry . . . . The harbor of my mind is an open bay, the only access to the island of my Self . . . .[3]

The concept of one's mind being a harbor is a wonderful analogy, because it's a great representation of the way our minds work. Holding onto grudges, resentments, hurt feelings, passing judgments, and being critical: these are all negative thoughts that we need to eliminate. When negative thoughts such as these enter your mind, what are you going to do about it? Imagine yourself as the harbormaster. Letting go of such negative thoughts is liberating, although it can be hard to do. After all, it has taken years, if not decades, to establish your way of thinking. So it's going to take time to change it, too. It takes practice, so don't try it only for a week, then give up and decide, "It doesn't work!"

The first step is to *become conscious* that you are harboring negative thoughts. The second is to catch yourself *while* you're doing it. The more you recognize it, the more quickly you'll be able to catch yourself, and then, you might be able to stop yourself *before* you do it. Once you recognize you're about to harbor a negative thought, and *choose* not to do it, that's where the real freedom comes in. You're about to go down that negative path, but then you choose another direction. It may help to realize that you don't need to replay that scenario in your head again. It's destructive and unhealthy. Elizabeth Gilbert decided to make her mind a "peaceful harbor:"

This is a peaceful harbor, the entryway to a fine and proud island that is only now beginning to cultivate tranquility. If you can abide by these new laws, my dear thoughts, then you are welcome in my mind – otherwise, I shall turn you all back toward the sea from whence you came.[4]

Become your own harbormaster. Turn *your* mind into a peaceful harbor and experience the happiness of being free of negative thoughts!

I heard of a schoolteacher who conducted an exercise on controlling one's thoughts with her class. She asked her students to look around the room and find all the things they could that were green. After a few minutes, she told them to close their eyes. Next she asked the class to tell her all the things they saw that were red. They couldn't do it! They had focused so closely on looking for green, they didn't notice the red things. It's the same way with gratitude. When we only focus on what we don't have, pretty soon that's all we see. If instead we focus our thoughts on our many blessings, we will become more aware of them, more grateful, and ultimately, happier.

An old Cherokee once said, "My son, there is a battle between two wolves inside us all. One is Evil. It is anger, jealousy, greed, resentment, inferiority, lies, & ego. The other is Good. It is joy, peace, love, hope, humility, kindness, empathy, & truth." The boy thought about it, and asked, "Grandfather, which wolf wins?" The old man quietly replied, "The one you feed."
—Cherokee legend

University of Adversity

> *A smooth sea never made a skillful mariner.*
> —Unknown

We all have to deal with troubles at one time or another. None of us will pass through this mortal existence unscathed. Part of the human experience is to face challenges and trials. If they are faced with courage and faith, they can help us to grow in ways that *nothing else* can.

> *I am more and more convinced that our happiness or our unhappiness depends far more on the way we meet the events of life than on the nature of those events themselves.*
> —Karl Wilhelm von Humboldt

Most of us don't see adversity as a blessing. We fight it, hate it, worry about it, and stress over it. Corrie Ten Boom's attitude, discussed previously, was an exception to this norm. It may be worth reflecting upon some of the adversity you've had in your life and asking yourself the question, "Where is the blessing in what happened?" For some of you it may be easily recognized, and for others it may lead to a wonderful discovery. Adversity makes us stronger, more compassionate towards others experiencing trials; it makes us wiser, and helps us appreciate life more.

There is opposition in all aspects of this life. But that opposition can also help us to recognize our blessings. Without sadness, we wouldn't recognize joy. Without pain, we wouldn't understand pleasure. After illness, we appreciate much more our good health.

Nobody escapes this life with only "smooth sailing." And it's important to recognize the times when we *are* experiencing "smooth sailing" to appreciate them.

> *The way I see it, if you want the rainbow, you gotta put up with the rain!*
> —**Dolly Parton, I Am a Rainbow**

Can we be happy while we're suffering? The truth is, yes, we can. If we waited for the perfect day when every conflict was resolved, every debt was repaid, and every problem was eliminated, then we would have put off happiness indefinitely. My father died rather suddenly when I was 37, most likely from a "broken heart." I don't think he ever truly recovered from the loss of my mom. As I worked through my grief, I discovered that I could still smile, and even laugh, as I reminisced about my parents. Of course, it helped to have a loving family and friends. But in the end, it is *our own attitude* that will determine what life we're going to live.

There is a point to the adversity in our lives; what "doesn't kill us" truly does make us stronger. If we choose to grow from our setbacks, we will be prepared to meet other disappointments with greater peace and optimism. We will be blessed with greater compassion, and insights that will allow us to help others facing similar situations. If we use the adversity in our lives to our advantage, it will be a positive thing.

> *I am not what has happened to me.*
> *I am what I choose to become.*
> —**Carl Jung**

If we can recognize the positive events going on in our lives *while* we're in the middle of a challenge, we will survive the experience with peace, rather than worry or stress. I mentioned in Chapter One my friend Jan who battled Non-Hodgkin Lymphoma for two years. Although she had a great attitude and was determined to beat the disease, she still occasionally had times when she felt a little bit discouraged, tired of the ravages of the chemotherapy and the tremendous disruption cancer was causing in her life. She noticed that whenever she needed a "lift," something would happen to provide it. A loving card arrived in the mail; a friend from far away telephoned to talk; somebody offered to take care of her two young children for a few hours; or a neighbor would drop by with flowers; there was always something. She is a religious person, and viewed these events as the hand of God in her life. She believed that God was helping her through other people, who were acting as some of His angels. That perspective made a huge difference in the way she viewed the experience. She felt God was aware of her suffering, He loved her, and He was sending help. The key was in being able to recognize those positive experiences in the midst of a very trying time.

A Sunday school teacher once conducted an interesting experiment during a class she was teaching on gratitude. She handed everyone a piece of paper and asked them to write down the 3 or 4 most difficult trials they were experiencing at the moment. The students were then asked to fold up their papers and put them in a basket. The basket was passed around the classroom, and everyone drew out a paper not their own. The teacher asked the class to consider the trials on the piece of paper they had just drawn, and whether they would trade their own trials for the ones on the paper. Asking for a show of hands of those who would take on the new trials in exchange for having theirs removed, *not one person* in the class raised their hand. Everyone was more comfortable with their own problems.

The way we endure the trials and challenges of life will be directly affected by our attitude. If we see hardships as stumbling blocks designed to impede our personal happiness, then we will be unhappy. If instead we see obstacles as opportunities for growth, the possibilities are limitless! As stated by Orson Whitney,

> No pain that we suffer, no trial that we experience is wasted. It ministers to our education, to the development of such qualities as patience, faith, fortitude and humility. All that we suffer and all that we endure, especially when we endure it patiently, builds up our characters, purifies our hearts, expands our souls, and makes us more tender and charitable . . .

Faith vs. Fear

When you are going through something hard and wonder where God is, remember the teacher is always quiet during a test.
—Unknown

All human emotions find their genesis in either the "faith camp," or the "fear camp." Stress, anxieties, depression, pessimism, discouragement, anger, loneliness and mistrust are all members of the fear camp. A recent national survey found that 75 percent of Americans are stressed, anxious and angry.

Undoubtedly, every one of us has "visited" the fear camp at least occasionally in our lifetime. The point is not that we shouldn't be fearful or that we shouldn't set foot in the fear camp. It is part of the human experience and is entirely normal. The point is that we don't have to *remain there* permanently. In fact, it really should be one of our goals to make shorter "visits" to the fear camp.

Worry will not strip tomorrow of its burdens,
it will strip today of its joy.
—www.lifebuzz.com[5]

If, for example, a person is generally feeling stressed for months at a time, maybe they can reduce it to a few weeks. If feelings of inadequacy ruled their life for weeks at a time, how much would their life improve if that could be reduced to just a few days? Instead of feeling discouraged for days on end, try wallowing in the muck for just one day.

How do we get out of the fear camp? The answer is by visiting the "faith camp" – by having faith. Worrying is actually having a lack of faith. Our lives don't need to be left to chance. We do have a choice to make, and choosing faith will have the greatest positive impact on how we live. Even though it's difficult, choosing faith immediately eliminates the fear. If we want to go from just surviving to thriving, faith is the only way! How do we visit the "Faith Camp?" Sometimes we can't get there by ourselves, no matter how hard we try. It may take active prayer and meditation, appealing to God or your higher power, to restore that peace to your heart that everything is going to be okay, everything is going to turn out all right.

> *Faith is taking the first step even when you can't see the whole staircase.*
> —**Dr. Martin Luther King, Jr.**

Some of the attributes found in the faith camp include hope, optimism, security, confidence, trust, happiness and peace. When "visiting" the faith camp, we are comforted. Faith is remaining at peace, even while in the middle of the storm. When everything seems to go wrong; when our dreams, aspirations, expectations or plans go awry, will we choose fear? Or will we consciously choose to have faith that things will turn out all right? The happy person chooses faith over fear and enjoys the wonderful benefits of doing so.

> **The happy person chooses faith over fear and enjoys the wonderful benefits of doing so.**

> *Worrying is like praying for what you don't want.*
> —**Unknown**

Appreciate what you have – while you have it!

Sometimes a crisis can actually help us to become more focused on how grateful our perspective should be. There's an old saying: "You don't know what you've got, 'til it's gone." We'll get so much more pleasure from life if we recognize and appreciate what we truly have – before we lose people or things we love!

A dear friend's father, Stanton, had a heart attack. It was 1978, and cardiac bypass surgery was a fairly new procedure. When Stanton and his wife Marion were told he needed a quadruple heart bypass operation, they were concerned and frightened. During the procedure, they were told, doctors would have to stop his heart from beating, and then re-start it near the end of the surgery. There was a risk they wouldn't be able to re-start it. Up until this point in time, Marion was bothered whenever Stanton left his dirty socks on the floor. She hated picking them up. Yet when Stanton entered the hospital, her perspective completely changed. She realized how grateful she was to be able to pick up those dirty socks – because it meant she still had her beloved husband. Marion was smart – she placed tremendous value on her relationship with Stanton, *while* he was still alive.

High school math teaches the concept that every equation has a converse. The converse is when the elements of a proposition are reversed. It's the same in life: for every problem, there's always a converse. As the poem quoted previously says, when our teenagers complain about helping with the dishes – we can be thankful they're home with us, instead of out on the streets. If there's a mess to clean up after a party, we can be grateful we were surrounded by friends.

Count your blessings!

> *I have sometimes been wildly, despairingly, acutely miserable, but through it all I still know quite certainly that just to be alive is a grand thing.*
> —**Agatha Christie**

A man who personifies this principle is my colleague, Dr. Terry Lyles. He's had a highly successful career, and is widely known as "America's stress doctor." Some time ago, the two of us had an opportunity to provide leadership training for the U.S. Air Force. In one of those classes he shared a very personal family heartache: his oldest son is afflicted with a devastating disease that prevents him from being able to do anything for himself. The disease struck when he was a very young child, but against all odds, he's still alive and now in his twenties. In terms of feeling gratitude, Dr. Lyles shared what he does every morning: when he gets out of bed, his first thought is, "I'm thankful I can put my feet on the floor, because my son can't." When he eats breakfast, he's grateful he can hold a spoon in his hand and feed himself, because his son can't. Dr. Lyles is grateful for many things that the rest of us may take for granted. He has realized it's a key part of the formula for being happy.

The following passage has some interesting statistics to consider:

> If you have food in the refrigerator, clothes on your back, a roof overhead and a place to sleep ... you are richer than 75% of this world.
>
> If you have money in the bank, in your wallet, and spare change in a dish someplace ... you are among the top 8% of the world's wealthy.
>
> If you woke up this morning with more health than illness ... you are more blessed than the million who will not survive this week.
>
> If you have never experienced the danger of battle, the loneliness of imprisonment, the agony of torture, or the pangs of starvation... you are ahead of 500 million people in the world.

If you can attend a church meeting without fear of harassment, arrest, torture, or death ... you are more blessed than three billion people in the world.

If your parents are still alive and still married ... you are very rare, even in the United States.

If you hold up your head with a smile on your face and are truly thankful ... you are blessed because the majority can, but most do not.

If you can hold someone's hand, hug them or even touch them on the shoulder ... you are blessed because you can offer healing touch.

If you can read this message, you are more blessed than over two billion people in the world that cannot read at all.

Have a good day, and count your blessings!

—Author unknown

If you start spending time each day counting your blessings, without a doubt that habit will change your perspective on life. It's a great – and easy – beginning toward having an "attitude of gratitude!"

What's the Attitude Behind Your Actions?

We do a lot of things out of duty. But what if we change our attitude? Decide to take out the garbage because we love our family – instead of taking out the garbage "because if I don't, my dad/mom/wife will get mad at me." As discussed in Chapter Two, most actions are motivated by pain, anger, fear, duty, or love. If you're motivated by anything other than love, it's very draining. It takes a lot of energy to do things because you fear the consequences if you don't do it, or if you are doing it resentfully. If you're acting out of a sense of duty, it's a good start – at least you're doing it! You may still expend a lot of extra energy – not as much as when the action is pain, anger or fear-based – but if your action is based on love, it seems so much easier, it's almost effortless.

Stop reading right now, and think about the last time you did something out of love for somebody. Let the feelings play out in your heart and mind. Think about it for a few minutes. . .

When "Less" is "More"

> *It's pretty hard to tell what does bring happiness; poverty and wealth have both failed.*
> —**Ken Hubbard** (Humorist and journalist)

Is having more wealth or more possessions the key to happiness? Have we been happy when we've had more STUFF? Of course we all need the basic necessities of life: food, water, clothing, and shelter. But how much more than that do we *really* need? We sometimes accumulate so much Stuff we have to rent a storage unit to store it all! Oftentimes, people judge one another by the amount of Stuff they have. Those who possess a big house, a new car, or a boat are perceived as being much happier than those who don't have those things. While those people may be happy, it will be *in spite of* their possessions, not because of them. Possessions can actually weigh us down and detract from our happiness. How many hours a week do you have to work to pay for your luxuries and their incidental associated costs? Do they distract you from the things that are truly important in your life – like your relationships with family and friends? What is the *real* cost to own so much *Stuff*?

> *We tend to forget that happiness doesn't come as a result of getting something we don't have, but rather of recognizing and appreciating what we do have.*
> —**Frederick Keonig**

When we have a grateful heart for what we *do* have, instead of focusing on what we *don't* have, *that's* when we'll be the happiest. When buying a new car, it's exciting in the beginning. But that excitement isn't true, long-term happiness. In fact, that initial pumped-up feeling will eventually dissipate…especially after the first dent!

If wealth and possessions were necessary for happiness, then happy people would truly be rare. A certain amount of money and possessions provide freedom, from which we derive pleasure, but "Stuff" is not where long-lasting happiness lies. The old adage that "money can't buy happiness" is true. No one is excluded from happiness because they don't have a lot of possessions. Real happiness comes from having gratitude in your heart and thankfulness in your soul. And the beauty of it is that *it is available to all of us!* It just takes some work to develop it into a habit.

> *The happiest of people don't necessarily have the best of everything; they just make the most of everything that comes along their way."*
> —**Karen S. Magee**

Real happiness comes from having gratitude in your heart and thankfulness in your soul.

Points to Ponder:

1. Once gratitude becomes entrenched in our mind, heart, and soul, the possibilities of a great life are endless.
2. Possessions don't lead to happiness.
3. We can control our thoughts.

Questions to Consider:

1. How does being grateful affect your life?
2. Faith or fear: which will you choose today?

Take Action

1. Why not start the gratitude habit right here and now? In the space below, write down ten things you are grateful for.

1. _____
2. _____
3. _____
4. _____
5. _____
6. _____
7. _____
8. _____
9. _____
10. _____

2. **Developing the Habit: Starting a Gratitude Journal**

Now that you're beginning to think about the things you're grateful for, it's time to start a gratitude journal. You can start with the ten things you wrote above. They have to be in writing – not just in your mind! The process of writing them down releases endorphins in our brains. Although you can do this at night, I like to do it first thing in the morning. For me, it's like putting the key in the ignition and turning it on. It shapes my perspective for the coming day and helps me to start out uplifted, feeling grateful and happy for my life.

Your gratitude journal will become a place for remembering and appreciating all the things that are good in your life. Think of blessings you received; people you connected with; beautiful things you saw; something you learned; moments you felt God nearby. If you write them down, they will not be forgotten or unappreciated.

You may want to write about a relationship in your life that you treasure; or an idea of how you can bless a family member or friend today; acknowledge and appreciate your talents; reflect upon a favorite memory of a time spent with a loved one, or describe a favorite teacher who made a difference. Say a prayer of gratitude, without asking God for anything. All of these things will buoy your spirits and encourage an attitude of gratitude.

You may want to include in your gratitude journal special cards and notes you receive from friends or acquaintances, such as thank you notes or birthday cards that express love or appreciation for you. A friend of mine keeps such cards and notes in a box she calls her "silver box." Your gratitude journal will become something treasured, not only as a record of what a truly wonderful person you are, but also as something you can turn to in moments of sorrow or despair. Reading previous entries will always bring you comfort and validation. It will help you to keep your focus on the positive aspects of your life. You will begin to see yourself differently. As you write about the good things in your life, you may be surprised by how much you have to say! This journal will become a special place you can visit any time you need to feel better about yourself.

3. Eliminate Negative Thoughts.

When's the last time you thought, "I don't have time for that" or "I can't do that"? Write it down here:

_____

Now consider what happens if you change the question to a positive one such as, "How can I find time?" or "How can I make that happen?" Write down the possible answers here: _____

_____

The crucial difference is in how the thought is phrased. If you change the question, you change the path – the direction of your mind is different, and you will therefore come up with different answers. All kinds of possibilities will occur to you if you give your mind the opportunity to come up with creative solutions, responding to "how" questions, instead of closing the door on ideas by thinking "I can't."

4. Consider the last time you did something for someone out of love: who was the person, and what did you do for them?
Write it down:

_____

How did it make you feel? _____
Did it make you feel closer to that person? _____
Plan to again do something out of love for someone.
For whom will you do it? _____
What will you do? _____
When will you do it? _____

_____

Chapter Six
The Third Path: Extend Forgiveness

"Forgiveness is the attribute of the strong."
—*Ghandi*

SEVERAL YEARS AGO, THE WORLD'S OLDEST MARRIED COUPLE WAS interviewed about their marriage. They had been married an astounding 85 years! The husband was 105 years old, and his wife was 100, so they got married when they were 20 and 15, respectively. When asked separately about the key to the longevity of their marriage, they responded with the same answer: the most important factor was that they both said the words "I'm sorry" daily, and asked for forgiveness often.

I had my own experience with this principle in the early part of my marriage. My wife and I had just moved to a new state with our first baby, bought our first home, and I was looking for a job. It was a very stressful time in our lives. Complicating the situation were the factors that we had married later in life and had already established a lot of our personal habits. We came from very different cultural and family backgrounds, and we both have strong personalities. We realized early on that we needed to set some parameters when we had a difference of opinion. Otherwise, it would have been far too easy for us to arrive at the "point of no return" during our discussions – that's the point in an argument where a person loses self-control and says or does something they will later deeply regret. Of course they can apologize and be forgiven, but the injury may never be forgotten.

To prevent this from happening in our marriage, we agreed upon a time-out plan. We decided that before we got to the "point of no return" during an argument, we would each have the right to call a time-out. Just as a coach at a sporting event may take a time-out to change the momentum of a game, when we are angry – before we get emotionally hijacked – we may need to change the momentum of the situation. We further agreed that we could both go to our separate corners and pray to know whom, if either of us, was right. This strategy has worked well for us through the years.

One evening shortly after our move, we started to get into an argument. It wasn't long before we both realized that neither of us was willing to give an inch, and the "point of no return" was almost upon us and approaching at lightening speed! We decided to call a time-out and cool off before any permanent damage occurred. In my mind there was NO doubt that I was right! So as I retired to my corner I approached my prayer with full confidence that I would be vindicated. I was all ready to say, "Dear God, please let my wife know how wrong she is, tell her to apologize, I'll be the bigger person and accept, and everything will be good!" But before I even had a chance to plead my case, a very commanding voice said to me, "Go back and apologize to your wife *right now.*" Imagine my reaction to *this* development! Actually, I ignored it initially! A few moments later an even more powerful voice repeated, "Go back and apologize to your wife **now**!!!" I very reluctantly gave in, feeling quite cheated by this time-out/prayer strategy since I wasn't even given the chance to tell *my* side of the story. So reluctantly I headed back towards our bedroom, where I saw my wife exiting and walking towards me. Her arms were folded in front of her and from her overall demeanor, I gathered that she had not received the answer that I had hoped for. Preemptively I blurted out, "Honey, I'm sorry that I hurt your feelings! I don't know what I said or did to hurt you," (I was truly clueless,) "but I'm sorry! Will you forgive me?"

That was when the miracle happened. Her arms dropped and her entire countenance changed. She put her arms around me, started to cry and apologized as well! The beauty of it was that all the negative feelings ended on the spot. As we hugged, I had a real epiphany . . . almost like the clouds parted over my head and a ray of light came upon me. I heard a voice say, "Now, Elia, in life and in your marriage, would you rather be RIGHT or would you rather be HAPPY?"

At no previous time in my life had I ever received such valuable words of counsel. I still had my free will to choose between being right (which I had chosen most of my life) or being happy, which was really what I wanted deep down inside. The answer was *so* easy and came *so* fast: of course I'd rather be happy! It's been over twenty

If you're always the one who is right, it means that the other person is always wrong.

years, and I've been quickly apologizing ever since. Interestingly, the more I've apologized, the easier it has become to say, "I'm sorry," or "please forgive me." And it has been equally reciprocated by my wife.

The bottom line is, if you're always the one who is right, it means that the other person is always wrong. Even if you win a debate or an argument, what have you really won, if the other person is angry or hurt? The only winner is your ego, which is fueled by your pride. However, the losses in this scenario can be staggering: the loss of happiness, the loss of trust, and ultimately, the loss of love or friendship. Is being right worth that? Absolutely NOT!!!

Lack of Forgiveness: Choosing "The Dark Side"

Unless we live as hermits and have no contact with other people, we will at times experience pain caused by others. It may be the result of someone's mistake, a broken heart, an addiction, being abused as a child, or a failed business venture, to name a few examples. Some people are easily offended and unwilling to let go of hurts. **Forgiveness is a *choice*.** If a person says, "I cannot forgive you," they're actually saying that they *choose not* to forgive you.

> *Holding onto anger is like drinking poison and expecting the other person to die.*
> —**F. Dunas**

To forgive means to "set it aside," to not let it emotionally, mentally and physically upset you anymore. It doesn't mean that the action done doesn't matter, for it surely still could hurt, but it no longer negatively affects you and you can move on to heal and grow . . . to not stay stuck. A visual image of literally packaging it up and setting it aside may help you to "see" what to do.

For any relationship to be successful, forgiveness has to be both extended and received. I don't think *any* relationship can survive long-term without forgiveness.

Chapter Six: The Third Path: Extend Forgiveness

*Forgive others not because they deserve it,
but because you deserve peace!*
—**Unknown**

What are the root causes of refusing to forgive someone? They are not particularly desirable traits. If we choose not to forgive, we're being selfish, rather than selfless; prideful, not humble; unbending, instead of flexible; withholding love rather than giving it. Interestingly, as I've worked with people over the years, I've discovered that those who had a hard time forgiving others *almost always* had an inability to forgive themselves for their own mistakes.

What happens when we don't forgive? For one thing, we start feeling resentful. That's a heavy burden to carry around. If we never admit to being wrong and always blame the other person, it drives a wedge in our relationships. It will eventually destroy our relationships with the people we won't forgive and, sadly, it will harden our hearts. Failing to forgive is poison to our own souls. And holding that poison inside will have a direct impact on us. Eventually, a person who fails to forgive will be lonely and probably unhappy.

> Failing to forgive is poison to our own souls.

Why is Granting Forgiveness Difficult?

Pride can get in the way of extending forgiveness. It's easy to be angry when another person hurts us. It's really a matter of priorities, though. What's more important to us: our hurt feelings, or the friendship with the person who offended us? And if we don't extend forgiveness, aren't we also being controlling? Some people delude themselves with misconceptions like, "If I hold on to my anger, I still have the power," i.e., the control. Another misconception is "If I forgive them, they'll do it again." Especially in the case of an abusive or toxic relationship, forgiveness *does not* mean placing oneself in harm's way again. Forgiving someone does not mean that you will allow that person to inflict the same wrong upon you again. Setting firm boundaries is the healthier way to protect yourself, not holding on to your anger.

Gain Your Freedom

Every sixty seconds you spend angry, upset or mad, is a full minute of happiness you'll never get back.
—**Unknown**

Forgiving others brings great freedom! Forgiveness brings freedom from anger, pain, resentment and even from clinging to bad memories. When you haven't forgiven somebody else, you're still a hostage – either to your past experiences, or to that person: whether they're alive or not; whether they live in another state, next door, or in your own home. You're giving up your power. Instead, why not give up the anger, pain, resentment, or the desire to punish the other person?

Practicing Forgiveness

If you want to make peace with your enemy, you have to work with your enemy. Then he becomes your partner.
— **Nelson Mandela**

We practice so many things in life, but we don't practice forgiveness. Like anything else, forgiving others becomes easier with practice. How do we do it? We all know we're *supposed* to do it, but we don't *know how* to do it. It's not something that's taught in schools or even in churches. We're just told we need to forgive, but are not given the tools for how to do it.

Forgiveness begins with the desire to be free, to have a clean slate. When you look in the mirror, what kind of person do you want to be? The choice is clear: you can either be someone who forgives and moves on, or someone who holds on to grudges. When we hold a grudge, or don't forgive, we're unhappy. There's no way a person can hold onto a grudge and still be happy. When we forgive somebody, the negative energy's gone; then when we remember an event, we no longer have the same negative emotional reaction to it. We're free of it, not dwelling on it anymore. We can recognize, "Yes, that person did do that to me, but I've moved on; that was then, this is now, I wish them well." When we forgive, the hurt doesn't have a hold on us anymore.

The Process of Forgiveness

The following is a six-step process of forgiveness that can help us understand how to forgive someone who has hurt us:

> *In order to move on, you must understand why you felt what you did and why you no longer need to feel it.*
> —**Mitch Albom, Five People You Meet in Heaven**

1. Work through the pain. "Forgiveness involves working through, not avoiding . . . emotional pain."[1] The first step in the process of forgiving another is to become aware of the price we pay for *not* forgiving. As long as we hold on to a grudge, there will be emotional pain that continues to hurt us. It's forgiveness that lets us reduce that pain.

> It's impossible to withhold forgiveness and fully love somebody.

It's impossible to withhold forgiveness and fully love somebody.

Perhaps the price we're paying is missing out on a loving relationship. Withholding forgiveness is not a loving thing to do. As Dr. Gary Chapman stated in his book *The 5 Love Languages*,

> We can choose to live today free from the failures of yesterday. Forgiveness is not a feeling; it is a commitment. It is a choice to show mercy, not to hold the offense up against the offender. Forgiveness is an expression of love.[2]

When we forgive someone, our hearts open up. When we refuse to forgive another, our hearts close. It is that simple.

2. Let go of the pain. Once you've figured out the price of withholding forgiveness, the next step is to decide to let go of the hurt, anger, or resentment. If this seems impossible, talk with a close friend or relative, a trusted adviser or even a professional counselor, and ask them to help you move beyond the incident. Talking about it will help you put into perspective the cost of holding on to the pain.

Extending forgiveness face-to-face is ideal, but if you can't, you can start the process by writing a letter to the person who offended you, telling them exactly how you feel, and why you feel the way you do. For example,

> *Dear John, this letter is a long time coming. I've struggled with what happened between you and me. Even though there's been a lot of hurt, I'm ready, willing and choose to forgive you completely, because our relationship is important to me.*

If there is a high likelihood that the other person will continue to engage in the hurtful behavior, it may be appropriate to send a letter that extends forgiveness, but instead of indicating a desire to continue the relationship, concludes with something along the lines of:

> *"I hope that you will make better choices in the future. I wish you all the good things in life.*

Sign the letter. Read it out loud after you write it, perhaps to somebody who can help you along the process, like a trusted friend. The decision whether to send the letter or not should be very carefully thought-out. When you write that kind of a letter, don't send it right away. After all, this has been a long time coming – you don't have to do it immediately. Sometimes the choice is already made, such as when the person has moved away to an unknown location, or is dead. Or you may not want to reopen that door, because this person is toxic and you don't want to be in contact with them (toxic relationships will be discussed further in

Chapter Nine). In that case, find an environment that's safe, like with a close friend, and read it to them. Then just get rid of the letter, and you're done! I've been through this process with hundreds of clients who, after reading me their letter, hugged me as they left exclaiming, "Thank you! I feel like a thousand pounds has been lifted off me!" They no longer have to deal with the pain. They're done.

On the other hand, if this is someone who's important in your life and you want to have a better relationship with them, you may want to send the letter. Another alternative is to pick up the telephone. The words are easier to say to the other person once you've practiced them.

3. Plan a Strategy in Advance. With regard to some wrongs, you may need to have a strategy in mind for future encounters if the other person is inclined to continue to hurt you the same way. Consider the hypothetical example of a relative who borrowed $1,000 from you but never paid it back. They come to you and ask for money again. If you've forgiven them and have a strategy planned, your response might be something like this:

> "Sure! I'll be happy to loan you money again, as soon as you pay me back the $1,000 you owe me, plus interest!"

If you've forgiven them, you can respond with a smile on your face. If you haven't forgiven them, you might grab them by the throat, snarling "What the %#@$! are you doing in my house?!" There's an issue of trust in a situation like this. The other person didn't pay you back the first time. If they say, "I don't have it," then you can smile and answer with your prepared response of, "Well, that's my final offer. You pay me back, I'll be happy to loan you the money again." There's no anger, no hurt, just an acknowledgement that they haven't paid you back. And then they'll probably leave and not ask again. By planning in advance, you can avoid a lot of unpleasant emotions.

4. Don't Dwell on the Hurt. It's important to recognize that **extending forgiveness is a choice, not an emotion**. Some hurts, such as physical abuse or an adulterous affair can be extremely difficult to forgive. The pain caused by such wrongs can continue for many years.

> It is not about reconciling with the person. That is a confusion that is rampant in our culture, that if I forgive I have to be reconciled to the person I'm forgiving. It is more like giving up the perceived right to get even. It's like giving up the attitude, 'You owe me.'"[3]

Nor does putting the negative memory out of your mind necessarily mean you'll forget the wrong forever. Some things simply can't be forgotten, such as when a loved one has been killed by someone in a car accident. **The key is not to dwell on the offense.** It can help to feel empathy for the person who has hurt you. For my friend Gary, this was crucial to his figuring out how to forgive his brother-in-law, who had murdered Gary's sister. Gary had prayed for help to forgive his brother-in-law, but didn't know how he could do so until the morning he first felt empathy for him. He realized that his brother-in-law, a snowboarder who deeply loved the outdoors and being in the mountains, would spend the rest of his life in an 8 x 8' prison cell. And even worse, he would also be in the "prison cell" of his own conscience – his own personal "hell," living with the realization of what he had done. That was the beginning of the process of forgiveness for Gary. A part of being empathetic is recognizing **there's more to the offender than their bad behavior.** The behavior that hurt you is only one part of who they are. However, forgiveness doesn't mean there will be a lack of consequences for the offender. In the example of Gary's brother-in-law, he will be in physical prison and also in the "prison" of his conscience for what he did, for the rest of his life. Nothing good will come from adding to that burden by hating him.

Once you have forgiveness in your heart, the hurt has no energy around it. Think of it as an event that's happened, but one that doesn't preoccupy your thoughts anymore. **Forgiveness gives you back power and control.** If you don't forgive, who *really* has the power? When we forgive we do not forget — it's just that the energy that's associated with that event or that person is diminished, or greatly diminished, until eventually it is nonexistent because you're not holding on to anything anymore. That's called peace.

> Once you have forgiveness in your heart, the hurt has no energy around it.

5. Be patient. "Be patient with yourself. Be patient with [the offender.] Human emotions are not things you can just switch on and off. . . Your feelings of hurt may linger longer than you would like."[4] If the process of forgiving takes longer than you would like it to, it isn't going to help things if you're beating yourself up over it.

6. Practice by starting small. Start with the people who are easier to forgive, where the forgiveness requires less energy. Then as you lighten your load, the big things will get easier. Forgiveness can be an acquired skill, but like any skill, you have to start practicing it. As soon as you forgive just one person, you will be amazed at how much lighter your load will become, and how ready you'll be to move on to the next one. My observation after having worked with numerous clients on this process is that after forgiving somebody, they gain a momentum, because it feels so good to them. Suddenly they want to forgive everybody, because they experience the benefits of forgiveness. Forgiveness is somewhat addictive! Eventually, we want to become "forgiveness *experts*!" Learn to forgive as quickly and frequently as possible, rather than carrying around the burden of all that hurt. We walk, talk and live surrounded by imperfect human beings - ourselves included - so it's *imperative* we become forgiveness experts! That contributes directly to one's happiness. The more we forgive, the lighter we will become, and the lighter we are, the happier we are.

The more anger towards the past you carry in your heart, the less capable you are of loving in the present.
—**Barbara de Angelis**

How Many Times Do We Need to Forgive?

In the Bible, we're told that if our brother sins against us, we need to forgive him not seven times, but "until seventy times seven" (Matthew 18:21-22). Undoubtedly that "seventy times seven" is a symbolic number. Making mistakes is part of the human condition. We all have made them, and will continue to make them, as long as we live . . . and it's *okay*! **People who are able to ask for forgiveness and who can be forgiving towards others, are much happier people.** Holding onto hurts leads to resentments. Letting go of hurt and anger leads to peace and freedom! Which will *you* choose? If you choose to let go, then why wait until later? Do it as quickly as possible and enjoy the benefits now!

Whom Are We Supposed to Forgive? Self-forgiveness is Crucial!

Over the years, I've had an opportunity to work closely with individuals who have hurt their families or loved ones through bad choices such as addictions, infidelity, and other destructive behaviors. There is a pattern with regard to forgiveness. Obviously, the individual needed first to make amends and ask forgiveness from the injured parties, be it their spouse, children, other family members, or someone else. Second, if they were religious, they had to ask for forgiveness from God and make a commitment to abstain from the hurtful behavior. Finally, there was one person left to forgive: *themselves*. Time and time again, this third step proved to be the hardest to accomplish.

Many years ago, my wife and I had visited a close relative who lived in another state. When it was time to go home, she offered to give us a ride to the airport. It was late at night, and somehow she ended up missing the airport exit and got turned around and confused. I honestly don't even remember if we missed the flight that night, but what I do remember is how hard she was on herself. She started sobbing as if she had done something terrible, and emotionally beat herself up. It was just a simple, honest mistake . . . the kind that each of us has often made in our lives. Eventually, we were able to reassure her enough to calm her down, but it took several hours of emotional anguish before she was able to see how hard she was being on herself, and forgive herself. If we're so self-critical when making trivial mistakes such as that one, imagine how much worse we are when we *really* mess up! It's time to lighten up and not be so hard on ourselves.

The act of self-forgiveness is undoubtedly *one of the most difficult* for most human beings to practice on a consistent basis. It has been my experience in my clinical practice that when someone has a hard time forgiving others, they almost *always* have greater difficulty forgiving themselves.

The best way to approach someone who seems to be unwilling to say "I'm sorry" in a relationship is actually to be very direct. I often will ask a troubled client, "Are you aware that you rarely, if ever, say 'please forgive me?'" If the answer is "yes," I ask, "Do you know *why* that's the case?" Most people genuinely have no idea why it is so difficult for them to apologize. I then ask them how often, secretly or otherwise, they forgive *themselves*. The usual response is one of silence, tears or an astounding acknowledgement: "never!"

Once I've helped clients connect their lack of forgiveness towards others with their lack of forgiveness towards themselves, then miracles begin to happen. In the end it becomes a win-win situation! People learn how to forgive themselves, and in turn become much more willing to forgive others. They have a softening of the heart. Once they get to that point, it becomes much easier for them to recognize that *they* have also caused others pain, and they are then able to *ask* for forgiveness as well.

How are we supposed to forgive ourselves?

Many people recognize at some level how important forgiveness is in life. But I don't know if they recognize how vitally important self-forgiveness is to their overall sense of happiness. I want to outline for you, step by step, how to forgive yourself. It does require work, but if you learn how to forgive yourself, then you've taken a huge step towards life-long happiness.

There's a specific process I've discovered that has been very helpful for people to learn *how* they can forgive themselves. When I work with someone who's having a difficult time forgiving themselves for something, I ask them to bring in their favorite picture of themselves as a child - when they were really young — from baby pictures to when they were 4, 5, or 6 years old. I want them to find their cutest childhood photograph — everybody has one – with a big smile, where they can see their face very clearly. I then ask them to look at that picture, and write down the attributes they see in that little person. These attributes tend to be pretty universal — they're describing an innocent little child. People typically write characteristics such as: "happy," "creative," "innocent," "pure," "cute," "loving," "trusting," "child of God," "adorable," "playful," "fun," "forgiving," and "full of love and light." Those attributes represent the best part of each person. It was before they made any mistakes, before they messed up. Before they hurt or disappointed others and themselves. This is the way that God sees each of us.

> **If you learn how to forgive yourself, then you've taken a huge step towards life-long happiness.**

Next, I ask the client to draw a line down the middle of the paper, then look in a mirror and write down what they see. Frequently the responses include words like "disappointed," "tired," "loser," "angry," "depressed," "stupid," "miserable," "stressed," and much worse. People can be *so* hard on themselves; they use the worst descriptions they can think of!

When the two lists are complete, I ask the client if they can look at the eyes in the photo of the little boy or little girl and say to them, "I do not forgive you. I'll never forgive you!" Time and again, it's impossible for them to do it. The response that frequently comes back, often said tearfully, is "that little boy/girl didn't do anything wrong." But those eyes are still *their* eyes: they're still the person in that picture. And if that little boy or girl asked them for forgiveness, it would absolutely happen. Because that little boy or girl is the best part of that person. It comes down to recognizing *who you really are*. It's impossible to withhold forgiveness from a child who asks, "Will you forgive me?" This process is the quickest and most profound way I've found to help an adult forgive themselves. It's a way we can be restored back to our better selves: to the person we *really* are!

If you need to forgive yourself for something, go through the process I've just described, and then plaster copies of that picture all over your life: in your car, on your computer, on your bathroom mirror. That little kid – your inner child – will become your guardian angel. In the Bible when Jesus was asked who would go to Heaven, to whom did He point? He said, "Become as a little child." He wasn't saying that we should become childish and immature; He said we should *become* as a little child. Look at the list you made to describe yourself in your childhood picture. What adult wouldn't want to have those attributes? That's where we find real happiness.

Choosing Not to be Offended

> *Weak people revenge. Strong people forgive.*
> *Intelligent people ignore.*
> —**Unknown**

Although it's a wonderful habit to forgive others and ourselves, we're even happier if we can avoid needing to forgive people in the first place. There is an old story about Buddha that goes as follows:

A great master sat on the side of the road outside of a village, cross-legged, quietly meditating. All of a sudden, a lunatic raced toward him, eyes wild, veins popping, foaming at the mouth. He began to berate the Master, making false accusations that he had committed horrendous deeds. The Master, however, remained completely calm, in control, and sat with his eyes closed, a smile on his face. The lunatic continued to make such a commotion, the villagers came out of their homes and were horrified that their Master was taking such abuse. They knew the things the crazy man was saying were not true. Finally, the lunatic realized he was getting no satisfaction from the Master, so he turned around and left.

The stunned villagers, astonished by what they had witnessed asked, "Master, we know that none of the things he said were true; why didn't you defend yourself?" After a while, he opened his eyes, turned to them, and instead of answering, asked them a simple question: "If someone offers you a gift, and you refuse the gift, to whom does that gift belong?" The people were mystified and bewildered, wondering what the Master was talking about.

He finally explained, "That man came down from the mountain and offered me the "gift" of verbal abuse. I didn't accept that gift; so he left with his abuse and venom just as he came, and I'm still free."

There are many opportunities to apply this same principle in our own lives. For example, if we're driving down the freeway and somebody flips us the bird, we can just smile and think, "They must be having a bad day." Then the incident won't be upsetting in the least. If we don't get angry, we don't need to forgive. Think of the freedom!

What About Asking For Forgiveness?

The flip side of the equation is that we all from time to time need to *ask* others to forgive *us*. Why is asking for forgiveness difficult? It actually takes a strong person to ask for forgiveness. It requires humility. Asking for forgiveness demonstrates a willingness to take responsibility for your behavior. . . More important, it validates the pain of the other person."[5] When you have offended a person you love, of course you want to validate their pain. Once you have learned to forgive yourself, and then extend forgiveness to others, you will experience a softening of the heart that will make it much easier for you to ask others for forgiveness. You'll have even more freedom!

> *To forgive is to set a prisoner free and discover that the prisoner was you.*
> —**Lewis B. Smedes**

Points to Ponder:
1. Forgiveness is a choice.
2. Forgiveness brings freedom!
3. Forgiveness takes practice.

Questions to Consider:
1. In what areas of your life have you not forgiven yourself?
2. Are there people you still need to forgive?

Take Action

1. Name all the people in your life that you have not forgiven as of this date. Start with the people who are easier to forgive, who require less energy.

_____
_____
_____
_____

2. With regard to each person, ask yourself "Why am I withholding forgiveness and holding on to these bad feelings?

    a. What are the benefits?

    _____

    b. What is the price I'm paying by not forgiving "X"?

    _____

    c. What resentments do I still have?

    _____

3. Commit to forgive each of these people, whether face-to-face (which is ideal), or in writing. Write down the plan for how you'll forgive each of them.

_____
_____
_____
_____

4. In what areas of your life have you not forgiven yourself?

    a. List specific incidents, things that you've done – and write them down. This is important!

_____
_____
_____
_____
_____

    b. Use the picture of you as a child to remind yourself who you really are, take the steps as explained in this chapter and then choose to forgive yourself for each of those incidents. Start with the easy ones to let go and forgive. (That way, you'll gain both momentum and practice in forgiving.) Now list the incidents (from part "a" above) for which you've forgiven yourself.

_____
_____
_____
_____
_____
_____
_____
_____

Chapter Seven
The Fourth Path: Follow Your Passion

"Happiness is neither virtue nor pleasure nor this thing nor that, but simply growth. We are happy when we are growing."
—*William Butler Yeats*

THE HAPPIEST PEOPLE I'VE EVER KNOWN ARE THOSE WHO SEEM TO HAVE discovered their "calling" in life. Imagine waking up every day with tons of energy, looking forward to whatever lies ahead because your life is so fulfilling! The key is to *love* what you do. **If you love doing something, it doesn't feel like work – it's a calling!**

A lot of the people I coach seem to struggle to find what makes them happy. Even those who are considered very successful by the world's standards, such as doctors, attorneys or business executives, often reach a so-called "mid-life crisis." Despite their success, they don't feel fulfilled. There are countless examples of celebrities who make millions of dollars a year, are adored by the public, and have all the perks of fame, yet seem to be miserable. None of these people have found their true calling in life. How do you discover your true calling in life? Following are a few strategies that can help you figure it out.

Ponder and Reflect

Discovering your passion - the pursuit that brings you joy and energy - is not always an easy task, but it is *never* too late to start living the life you once imagined in your youth. And you don't need to wait for the situation to become a crisis. Why not engage in a *"mid-life reflection"* instead of having a "mid-life crisis?" **It's vitally important to take the time occasionally to reflect on what your life is all about.** What contributions are you making to those around you? What is your purpose in this life? What do you most love doing? Maybe it's time to "reinvent" yourself. I often ask clients, "Are you a human being or a human 'becoming'?"

What Made You Happy When You Were Young? It may help to reflect back upon an earlier time in your life. What did you enjoy doing when you were young? What made you feel good about yourself? What were your natural gifts? Have you developed those as an adult?

The earliest indicator that I would end up in my profession happened during middle school. Many of my friends confided in me and asked for advice. I didn't have any training, of course, but my advice usually seemed to work out. I was always happy when they came back to thank me. There was something about helping others and seeing them feel better that made me feel good. Long before I knew I could actually make a living by giving people advice, I was hooked.

Remember your dreams and aspirations when you were young. Are they still important to you? If so, how can you fulfill them now? It's simple, really:

adapt them to your current situation. If you wanted to be a professional soccer player, join an adult soccer league. If you wanted to be an artist, take an art class through a local college or community continuing education program. It's never too late to find a way to fulfill those dreams. It's been said that, "Everything begins with an idea." So start dreaming! No matter what stage you are at in life, you can continue learning new things, you can develop your passions, and in doing so you'll make your life more meaningful.

What Are Your Dreams Now? I often meet people who are burned out. They are merely going through the motions of each day. In essence, they are just surviving. They look like they're exhausted by their lives. I ask them, "If you had a magic wand and could create your life the way you've always wanted it to be, what would it look like? Don't limit yourself! **If you dream it, it can happen!"**

What Are Your Passions? People who pursue their passions are happy people. I grew up in Southern California, and I was a major sports fanatic. I remember watching the great Lakers basketball player, the legendary Earvin "Magic" Johnson, when he was a rookie. In his first game playing in the NBA, his teammate Kareem Abdul-Jabbar was the league MVP and a perennial all-star. The Lakers won the game at the buzzer as Kareem took his final shot. Magic's reaction was to jump up and hug him! This was just one game – there are 82 in the regular season – but when asked about it, Magic responded: "You don't understand! I love this! I'd do it even if they weren't paying me!" His excitement was palpable. Even though he had made it into the NBA, had won many awards while playing in college, and had received many accolades over the years, he was never bored or took it for granted - because it was his passion.

When Johnson decided to retire because he became infected with the HIV virus, he became a tremendously successful businessman, largely because of the way he goes about things. He continued to have a contagious smile and a positive attitude, despite the death sentence that used to accompany HIV infection. He has worked on building the inner city of L.A., blessing the communities of those who are disadvantaged. He maintains the same vigor and optimism that he had as a superstar in basketball, finding joy in whatever he does. Some professional athletes retire, put up their feet and grow fat. Magic Johnson is a great example of somebody who reinvented himself instead.

The Examples of Others. You may find inspiration by thinking of the people you most admire. What characteristics do they possess? Look around and see if there's someone else doing something *you* want to do. Albert Schweitzer said, "Example is not the main thing in influencing others. It's the only thing." Almost every successful person has been inspired by somebody, whether their career is in acting, sports, business, or some other field.

> *Inspiration is everywhere, but you have to be looking.*
> —**Jane Pauley**

It's Never Too Late. We don't always pursue – or may not even discover – our passions until later in life. It's never too late to start! In 2010, a 99-year-old World War II veteran named Akasease Kofi Boakye Yiadom became the world's oldest person to receive a college diploma. He enrolled in the Presbyterian University College business school in Ghana when he was 96, and graduated in April 2010. Mr. Yiadom's attitude is inspirational because he understands that it's never too late to continue learning and growing:

> "Education has no end," Yiadom told CNN. "As far as your brain can work alright, your eyes can see alright, and your ears can hear alright, if you go to school you can learn."[1]

So don't let your age or the passage of years hold you back!

> ***Never give up on a dream just because of the time it will take to accomplish it. The time will pass anyway.***
> ***—Earl Nightingale***

It's Not Only About You! Any work that benefits *only* you will never make you truly happy. Find what you enjoy, but make sure the benefits or blessings of your calling can have a positive impact on at least one other person. That positive impact will bring you joy. If your true calling enables you to leave the world a better place, you will find great personal fulfillment and satisfaction – and happiness!

I have a friend who used to be an executive at a big company. He was a very "left brain" kind of guy – a financial wizard – and he'd made a lot of money. When his company was recently merged with another large company, he was laid off. I asked him what he was going to do next (he was in his 40's), and he responded, "I've always liked baking. I'm going to buy this bakery and run it." When he first told me about his plans, I was shocked! He was always wearing a suit, going to meetings with other high-powered business people, and traveling the world. Envisioning him behind a bakery counter wearing an apron seemed completely far-fetched! He explained that he wanted to spend more time with his wife and kids. It was to be a family affair, with everyone working together side by side.

He knows how to run a business, and I have no doubt that even though he is taking on this bakery almost as a hobby, it will be a very successful enterprise. More importantly, he will be doing something he's always dreamed about, and it will benefit his whole family, bringing them closer together.

Changing Your Course

Reinvent Your Life. People who are not pursuing their true callings (either in their main career or as an avocation) frequently get to "the end of their rope," and feel unfulfilled. There is a process that can help a person in this situation to "reinvent" their life, and design it the way they've always wanted it to be. Jinny S. Ditzler describes a great process in her book *Your Best Year Yet*.[2] A few simple steps can help a person make meaningful changes that will bring greater happiness to their life. The process is laid out in the Take Action section at the end of this chapter, but as you're reading this, take the steps in your mind:

First, reflect back upon the last 12 months, 10 years, or even the last 25 years of your life, depending on how deep you want to go. Focus on the things that you feel proud of, your accomplishments, and the things that you did well. It's important for us to acknowledge some of the positive things that have happened in our lives. How often do we have a to-do list of 10 things, get 7 of them done, and then beat ourselves up for the 3 things we didn't do? That's human nature. Instead, we should be glad for the things we *did* accomplish. We all need to recharge our personal "batteries" from time to time. Reflecting upon the things we're proud of is one way of doing that.

Consider what you can learn from your successes. They will tell you what you already know how to do. If you take a closer look at your successes, asking questions like "How did I achieve that?" "Why was I successful at that?" and "What did I do to make that happen?" can help you figure out how to apply the principles that resulted in a success to other areas of your life.

Next, looking back at that same time period, think about some of your biggest setbacks, disappointments, or things that didn't work out. The things we can learn from our failures are our *potential* lessons. If we don't learn from our failures, they'll probably happen again. Take, as an example, my own situation that culminated in a health crisis. I was working so hard, it actually made me physically ill. There were signs that I was getting sick, if I had paid attention to them, but I didn't. And so the situation continued, and the second year it was a lot worse, until it was so painful it was unbearable. I ended up in the hospital, having surgery. Then I was forced to make changes.

> If we don't learn from our failures, they'll probably happen again.

Are You Fulfilled by the Roles you Play in Life? It may help you to discover your true calling if you consider things from a slightly different perspective: think about the different roles you play in life. We all wear a lot of hats: mother/father, daughter/son, sister/brother, friend, employee, or caretaker, for example. Evaluate how well you are fulfilling the roles in your life. Is it time to focus more on a role you have always wanted to play? What is it? How can you pursue it? Maybe you'll need to eliminate or at least reduce another role. Can someone else assist you with one of your roles (for example, by carpooling) so you have more time and ability to focus on other roles you play or want to play?

If you were to make an improvement in one of these areas of your life, which one would have the greatest impact in your life? Determine where you are the strongest – where you are doing okay – and where you need to focus some energy. For example, if you were unemployed during the last year, you probably need to focus on getting a job. That will affect everything else you do. Maybe you haven't talked to your parents for 15 years. If you were to reconcile with them and heal the hurt, what kind of an impact would that have? It's not that you should neglect the other areas of your life, but make improving this one area your top priority.

Evaluating the roles in your life might even motivate you to adopt a *new* role. If you became an empty nester, your role as a mother/father has diminished, but you can create a new role for yourself. You can go back to school, travel and see the world, or perhaps develop a new skill or talent. We occasionally need to make room for a new role in our lives.

Trying Something New Adopting a New Role. Whether we plot a course, have goals and pursue them (i.e., whether we **live our lives, or simply exist** and allow things to happen to us), life changes constantly and *so can we!* There are endless possibilities for a new start. When we take control of the direction of our lives by *doing*, the resulting growth generates feelings of competence and confidence. Each of us learns the depth of our capabilities by exploring and by trying new things. The more we know, the less scary the world is, the more fulfilling our lives become, and the more opportunities will arise. But if we never try anything, we will have failed to reach our greatest potential.

Michelangelo said it best:

> The greater danger for most of us lies not in setting our aim too high and falling short; but in setting our aim too low, and achieving our mark.
>
> —Michelangelo di Lodovico Buonarroti Simoni

Frequently referred to as the "creator of the Renaissance," Michelangelo was a painter, sculptor, architect, poet, and engineer, and achieved tremendous accomplishments during his lifetime in every one of those disciplines. Even so, one of his most famous remarks was, "I am still learning."

Is there a role that you haven't played before that you've always wanted to play? Even if adopting that role seems impossible or improbable, you should pursue it.

In the "Take Action" Section of this chapter, there will be a place for you to write down a new role for yourself. By writing it down, you will bring it to the forefront of your consciousness. You will begin to recognize opportunities and people that may help you achieve that goal, which in the past you might not have seen. It may be so far out of your comfort zone, you may not have any idea how to make it happen – but by putting it down on paper, doors will open up for you. I know this to be true from personal experience.

> "I am still learning."

> *Goals you don't pursue aren't goals, they're dreams, and dreams only make you happy when you're dreaming.*
> —Jeff Haden

Even a Small Change Can Make a Difference. A new role doesn't necessarily mean you have to make a big change, like a career change. But if you're stuck in a difficult situation, such as being a single parent, or working at a job you don't like but cannot leave, you can still find fulfillment in another area of your life and thereby increase your overall happiness.

> You can learn even more from your disappointments (your "potential" lessons) than you learn from your successes.

If you've had disappointments, consider what you'd like to do differently to avoid feeling the same way next year. You can learn even more from your disappointments (your "potential" lessons) than you learn from your successes. That's the beauty of potential lessons! If you change just one negative factor, such as a self-defeating behavior, and the course of your life changes by just a few "degrees" – it can have a profound impact on the level of your happiness.

Dieter F. Uchtdorf, a former airline executive once told the story of a tragic plane crash that occurred because of a slight change in course:

> "In 1979 a large passenger jet with 257 people on board left New Zealand for a sightseeing flight to Antarctica and back. Unknown to the pilots, however, someone had modified the flight coordinates by a mere two degrees. This error placed the aircraft 28 miles (45 km) to the east of

where the pilots assumed they were. As they approached Antarctica, the pilots descended to a lower altitude to give the passengers a better look at the landscape. Although both were experienced pilots, neither had made this particular flight before, and they had no way of knowing that the incorrect coordinates had placed them directly in the path of Mount Erebus, an active volcano that rises from the frozen landscape to a height of more than 12,000 feet (3,700 m).

As the pilots flew onward, the white of the snow and ice covering the volcano blended with the white of the clouds above, making it appear as though they were flying over flat ground. By the time the instruments sounded the warning that the ground was rising fast toward them, it was too late. The airplane crashed into the side of the volcano, killing everyone on board.

It was a terrible tragedy brought on by a minor error—a matter of only a few degrees.[3]

This principle is equally true of positive changes: if we make even a small positive adjustment in our lives, we can be someplace better next year. If we can do just one thing to avoid something we did last year that led to a failure, it can make a great improvement in our life. Maybe it's going to bed at 10:00 p.m., instead of staying up until midnight, then waking up sleep-deprived and cranky the next day. Getting two more hours of sleep and waking up energized and rejuvenated would make an incredible difference in a person's life! It could be a commitment not to drink, or a decision to read good books instead of watching television.

Whatever change you make, that one adjustment can have a profound, positive impact in your life. So consider what you've learned from your accomplishments and disappointments, and decide where an adjustment will have the biggest influence in changing the course of your life.

Do Something You Excel at as Often as Possible. When you do something you're good at frequently, it will give you a sense of success, and a sense of accomplishment – and that in itself will make you feel happier. The more you enjoy what you do and the more fulfilled you feel by what you do, then the happier you will be.

On the other hand, it's probably not practical to do only the things you love. We all need to venture out of our comfort zones, because that's where growth and development happen. But we can find ways to spend *more* time doing what we love, by delegating some of our responsibilities: we can get others to help us with the tasks we enjoy less.

Get Expert Advice. A great strategy when we want to learn something new is to go to an expert, interview somebody who's already successful at it. The wonderful thing is, most people don't mind being consulted about their work. People generally enjoy mentoring others. It's satisfying for them to be able to give back to others by providing input to those who are seeking a similar career path.

Reflect Upon the Balance in your Life. In Chapter Four, we discussed the importance of having balance in our lives. Just as maintaining physical, emotional and spiritual balance is essential to our overall happiness, developing intellectually is also a crucial part of living a well-balanced life. Take some time to consider where you are intellectually, physically, emotionally, and spiritually. As physical, emotional and spiritual balance are discussed elsewhere in this book, only intellectual development is addressed in this chapter.

Intellectual Development

Pursuing intellectual development may be a key to finding your calling. As you learn new skills or gain additional knowledge, all kinds of opportunities can arise, and new possibilities may occur to you.

Our brains need to be "fed" in the same way our bodies do. In this age of immediately available information, stimulating our brains is not difficult. Following are some of the many ways we can "feed" our brains:

1) Formal education.
Probably the most obvious method of developing intellectually is to pursue a formal education. If you never obtained a college degree and you want one, there are ways you can get one now. A friend of mine recently turned 60, and she is working on getting her bachelor's degree from the university she attended for two years, before she married at age 20. It always bothered her that she had not graduated from college, so she is doing something about it now, after having raised four children. With online opportunities, college degrees are more accessible, and probably more affordable, than ever before.

Perhaps you would gain personal satisfaction or career advantages by pursuing an advanced degree. Maybe you'd simply enjoy taking a class at a community college to learn a new skill, or a new language, or learn about a field of study that has always interested you.

In graduate school, Dr. Terry Oleson was my clinical supervisor as I worked on my doctoral dissertation. At least one or two weekends out of every month he traveled someplace to take a seminar of some kind. Whenever he returned from a seminar, he'd share some of what he'd learned with me. One day I asked him why, when he already had so many degrees, he continued to attend so many seminars.

> "It keeps me young," he responded.
> "But all these things you go to," I persisted, "aren't they boring sometimes? Do you get anything out of them?"
> His answer has had a lasting impact on my life:

> "When I go to any workshop, any seminar, any class that I take, if I get one thing out of it that I can apply to my life that will improve the quality of my life or that of others, then I consider that workshop to be a success. There has never been a workshop that I believe was a waste of time. Maybe not all 8 hours were great – but if I got *one* thing out of it, it was a success."

2) Staying "current."

If pursuing additional formal education isn't an option for you right now, there still are almost endless opportunities for stimulating your brain. Since I was young, I have spent at least an hour every morning reading about current events in politics, business, sports, and entertainment. On days when I have more time, I may spend as long as three hours reading a newspaper or catching up on the news on the Internet. Doing this has blessed my life in multiple ways: it keeps me "in the loop" because I'm up to date on world events and other issues of interest; it has helped my mind to stay sharp; and it often helps me to connect with other people, talking about current events. I never know when the news items I learn about are going to be relevant. Sometimes the news is more profound, while at other times it is more light-hearted, as with sporting news or celebrity events. But by staying up with current events, every day my mind is intellectually fed and stimulated. I always want to know more! I never tire of learning new things. **There aren't many things in life we can do for so many years and not get tired of them.**

It's so easy to be distracted by mindless games, like some of the video games that preoccupy a lot of us but really don't contribute to one's overall growth as a person. Of course everyone needs an occasional "escape," but if you use that time for something with redeeming value – something that will stay with you and enhance your life – it will be a much more valuable and fulfilling use of your time, and it will bless your life by stimulating your brain.

3) Read books.

Reading good literature is another great way to stimulate your brain. My wife Sona loves to read the classics. She even enjoys books she has read before, because it's a very different experience to read a book when you're young than to do so as an adult. We see things differently at different times in life, and you may appreciate a book more as an adult than you did if you read it as a young teenager. You may benefit from joining a local book club. Book clubs have the added benefit of providing social interaction with others.

There are endless possibilities for us to continue learning! Take a class or seminar, learn a foreign language, travel, stay informed about current events, develop your talents, or listen to educational CDs. Almost everyone has access to a free public library or the Internet. You can learn about anything you want. Choose something you want to learn about, and go for it! The end result will be an accomplishment that will enrich your life, build your confidence and expand your world. It may even help you to be more profitable in your business, or more marketable if you're looking for a new job or career.

Whatever works for you, make sure that it becomes a regular part of your life: just like exercising and eating well, try to stimulate your brain. There is a thirst for knowledge in all of us. Just because it isn't a habit for you doesn't mean you don't have that thirst. I know that if you seek greater intellectual development, it will bless your life, as it has mine.

> *Education is the single most consistent and powerful instrument for the advancement of an individual and a people.*
> —Johnnetta B. Cole

Do a little "Spring Cleaning"

Discovering a new calling is exciting and life-enhancing! However, there's another part of the equation that's also important. That is to let go of "old stuff" or old dysfunctional patterns. Think of it as an intellectual or emotional "spring cleaning." To illustrate, imagine getting a new dining room set for your home. When the deliverymen show up and ask where the new set should go, if you were to respond, "Just crowd it in there with the old dining room set," that would seem ridiculous! It makes much more sense to sell the old set or give it away, before the new one is delivered.

When it comes to physical things, it makes perfect sense to make room for the new by getting rid of the old. How about old patterns and habits that are weighing us down? Why should we wait until next New Year's Day to make another resolution for change? Now is the very best time to eliminate one negative thought pattern or behavior and replace it with seeds of happiness and health. Consider which negative thought or behavior you are willing to let go of first, to replace it with something positive.

> **Now is the very best time to eliminate one negative thought pattern or behavior and replace it with seeds of happiness and health.**

Circumstances May Force a Change

There are an almost unlimited number of events that initially may be perceived as being negative (such as bankruptcy, job layoffs, illness, divorce, or the death of a spouse) but which can spur us to action. They can jolt us out of our comfort zones and require significant changes in direction. The trick is to view these events for what they truly are: opportunities.

Several years ago, I was working so hard and doing counseling at such an intense pace, it literally made me sick. I ended up in the hospital, and as I had plenty of time to "ponder and think," I realized the unrelenting workload had deeply and negatively affected my life. In order to regain my health, I had to make a change. I needed to reinvent my professional life so I could again find my inner peace. I vowed never again to become burned out from something I had once loved! The ensuing change has been a tremendous blessing. I would never before have imagined myself writing a weekly column, or traveling all over the country to doing executive coaching, leadership training and lecturing.

I have realized that everything I did in the first part of my life was a preparation for what I'm doing now. I love coaching people in their personal and professional lives. In helping others to move from just surviving, to thriving in their relationships, I have discovered a new calling in life. This principle applies to everybody. Everything you've done in your life up until this time is preparation for what you can do now! As Jane Pauley put it in her wonderful book *Your Life Calling: Reimagining the Rest of Your Life*, "I expect to be cycling in and out of reinvention for the rest of my healthy life. I believe that you never stop growing until you stop trying."[4]

> *Life is either a daring adventure or nothing at all.*
> —Helen Keller

What's Holding You Back?

> *The only man who makes no mistakes is the man who never does anything.*
> —Eleanor Roosevelt

Fear of Failure. One of the greatest fears people have – and it's universal – is the fear of failure. In many ways it stems from the fear of rejection. Successful people in life have learned to overcome their fear of failure. But for those who haven't overcome it, it stops them dead in their tracks. It can be debilitating and a major obstacle to happiness and success. Most people do not achieve a fraction of what they are capable of achieving because they are afraid to even *try* something new.

> *If you fell down yesterday, stand up today.*
> — H.G. Wells

How can we overcome our fear of failure? Each one of us has failed thousands of times in our lifetime! It started as early as when we learned how to walk. The first time we stood up and fell down, maybe hurt ourselves, we didn't give up. If we had, we'd still be crawling around the house at 40 years old! There was something that inspired us to keep on trying. We all have an **The only true failure is giving up.** innate ability to be persistent; some of us just need to re-discover it. It's very rare for anybody to start something new and think "I've got this down pat" the first time. Remember the first time you got behind the wheel of a car? It was pretty scary – yet now you don't even think twice about it, because you've mastered that skill. Once we've mastered something, it becomes second nature. You can apply this principle to anything. What's the fear that's in front of you *right now*? Remind yourself about when you learned to drive. It's through multiple failures that success comes. The only *true* failure is giving up. So keep trying!

> *Success is going from failure to failure without loss of enthusiasm.*
> —Winston Churchill

It's important to recognize failures as opportunities for learning. Oftentimes when people fail at a task, they feel like *they* are a failure. They personalize it. But as author William D. Brown once said, **"Failure is an event, never a person." I love this saying!**

Another strategy that can help overcome our fear of failure is to talk about how we're feeling. Expressing your fear to a trusted friend or family member can help build your confidence. Somehow, when we talk out loud about a fear to somebody, it loses its "power." If we keep our self-defeating thoughts to ourselves, however, because we're our own worst enemy, it's a lot harder to overcome them. Share it with somebody and your perspective will change. Another person can remind you of other times you struggled and overcame. We're all products of a series of successes in life. We just don't acknowledge them – we take them for granted.

> *Obstacles are those frightful things you see when you take your eyes off the goal.*
> —Henry Ford

Fear of Success. People often believe that they are undeserving of all the good things and recognition that come their way as a result of their accomplishments and successes. I've seen this condition frequently in people I've coached. If they have accomplished something but don't feel like they deserve it, they're very uncomfortable. They seem to think, "If people knew the *real* me, they wouldn't be making this big deal." Many are very uncomfortable with the limelight that comes with success. So they tend to self-sabotage themselves. Pick up a magazine in the grocery store any day and you'll see it: wealthy, successful, beautiful, extremely talented people whose lives are falling apart. Consciously or not, on some level they probably don't believe they deserve the success they've achieved. Chapter Three, "The First Path: Loving Yourself" discussed this issue. We don't have to know everything – and there isn't a person on earth who does! Don't forget to love yourself, and realize you don't need other people's approval to be yourself, and to succeed.

Maybe it's the way they were taught; sometimes that can come from one's upbringing. Were you told as a child that you weren't going to be a success, or that you were never going to amount to anything? If you have these kinds of feelings, perhaps it would be worth reflecting back upon your upbringing. What messages about success were taught in your home while you were growing up? What did your parents say about wealthy people, successful people? If they were negative messages, like "Rich people are snobs," you may have thought, "I don't want to be like them." But you don't have to embrace those negative messages anymore.

Fear of Change. The *only constant* in life is change. We generally like staying in our comfort zone because it's familiar, and perceived as being safe. People sometimes try to avoid changes at all costs because they're afraid to get out of their comfort zone. Yet that's the *only place* where growth exists. In essence, this entire book is geared toward getting you *out* of your comfort zone! But it's for a good purpose, because **growth leads to happiness**.

> *Man's mind, stretched to a new idea,*
> *never goes back to its original dimensions.*
> —**Oliver Wendell Holmes, Jr.**

Although it can be scary, sometimes the unknown can become a pleasant surprise. How many times have you tried something totally new, having some trepidation beforehand, even some fear, and it turned out much better than you had thought it would? Had you never gone outside of your comfort zone, you never would have experienced that.

People who are passionate about growing may be afraid of a change but they "go for it" anyway. To them, change is simply another way of **taking charge and living fully**. Don't be afraid, get out of your comfort zone, and I promise you will not be disappointed. You will grow!

> *If you really want to do something, you'll find a way.*
> *If you don't, you'll find an excuse.*
> —**Jim Rohn**

Finding Your Calling. If you want to find your true calling in life, this chapter has described some of the practical steps – a framework you can to use to examine your life. The lessons can be applied to your finances, to your work, to your family relationships; the possibilities are endless! Many of us do not take the time to do this self-reflection. But if we don't do it, we may find that we're merely *existing rather than living our lives*.

Gather up your courage and take that first step toward reinventing yourself. Jane Pauley stated it beautifully in *Your Life Calling: Reimagining the Rest of Your Life,* when she wrote, "Entering my late 50's, I knew that this time, if anything was going to happen *I'd have to make it happen myself."* [Emphasis added]. [5]

People who have accomplished a lot in life, who have contributed to humanity, have undoubtedly taken the time to withdraw from the "rat race," to go into a "cocoon," and to re-discover themselves. If we take the time away from our BUSY-ness to do this kind of introspection, I promise it will make a significant difference. It will change the course you are on for the better. It will inevitably have a positive impact on other people, too, which is one of the crucial aspects of true happiness. So start reinventing yourself . . . thrive, instead of survive ... and you'll love the results!

We must all suffer from one of two pains: the pain of discipline or the pain of regret. The difference is discipline weighs ounces while regret weighs tons.

—Jim Rohn

Points to ponder:

1. Discovering your calling will lead to happiness.
2. Getting out of your comfort zone brings growth.

Questions to consider:

1. Your Dreams, Past and Present

What were your dreams and aspirations when you were young?

1. _____
2. _____
3. _____

If those dreams are still important to you, how can you fulfill them now?

_____
_____
_____

What are your dreams now?

1. _____
2. _____
3. _____

What are you going to do to fulfill them?

_____
_____
_____

Take Action

II. Making a Course Adjustment

The following process is described in the book *Your Best Year Yet*, by Jinny Ditzler.[6]

1. Think about the last 12 months, 10 years, even 25 years of your life – depending on how deeply you want to get into it. Now write down all the things that you feel proud of and have accomplished; things you did well. It can be anything, ranging from "I paid off some debts," "I lost some weight," "I moved into my dream house," "I got married," "I got certified in something," "I did volunteer work;" whatever you can think of. Write them down.

A. _____

B. _____

C. _____

2. Look at the successes you wrote down above. What can you learn from them? Write down the reasons for your greatest success:

A. _____

B. _____

C. _____

3. Next, looking back at that same time period, write down some of the biggest setbacks, disappointments, or things that didn't work out. Whether it's a failed relationship, getting fired from a job, or not getting the promotion you thought you were going to get, the loss of a loved one, not being able to have a child, or getting into a car accident; whatever it is, write it down.

A. _____

B. _____

C. _____

4. What can you learn from those disappointments? Using the same principles that brought your greatest success, write down your potential lessons:

A. _____

B. _____

C. _____

5. Look at the different roles you play in life. Write them down below, and be sure to include the role of the self-caretaker.

_____

_____

_____

Assign a number between 1 and 10 to each of the roles you wrote down, to evaluate how well you are fulfilling those roles. 10 would indicate you're happy with the job you're doing; a 1 means you're pretty dissatisfied.

6. If you were to make an improvement in one of these areas of your life, which would have the greatest impact on your lifestyle? Look especially at the area where you gave yourself the lowest score. Determine where you are the strongest – where you are doing okay – and where you need to focus some energy. Write down the area of your life you want to improve – the area to be your main focus in the coming year.

_____

_____

7. Are there old patterns and habits that are weighing you down? Write down what you're going to let go of:

_____

_____

_____

III. Intellectual Development: What are you doing to stimulate intellectual development in your life? Are you taking adult education classes or working on getting a college degree or post-graduate degree? Do you read regularly? Are you working to enhance skills necessary for your career?

What would you like to see happen over the next year? _____
_____

Make an action plan using SMART goals and write it down here: _____
_____
_____

Chapter Eight
The Fifth Path: Nourish Your Spirit

"We're not human beings having a spiritual experience. We're spiritual beings having a human experience."
—*Pierre Teilhard de Chardin*

IF WE LOOK AT THE GREAT CULTURES THAT SURVIVED FOR CENTURIES, they all emphasized having a spiritual balance in life. In cultures that failed, such as one of the greatest empires - the Romans - the spiritual balance was gone. The carnal nature of man took over, and the result was decadence and debauchery that eventually destroyed their society.

There is a powerful connection between our minds, bodies and spirits. We can no more separate the mind from the body than we can separate the spirit from the body, or the spirit from the mind. Each aspect of our beings needs nourishment. Just as our bodies need rest, moderate exercise and healthy foods, and our minds need the stimulation of good books and learning new things, our spirits also have needs.

The crux of the matter is, *what* does a spirit need? This is not about a specific religion; the spirit that's inside of us is not boxed in by a particular religion. The spirit is *eternal*. It's the very essence of who we are – it is our *soul*. We each need to address our spiritual needs on a daily basis. If we ignore the spiritual part of our beings, we're ignoring a vital part of living.

> **If we ignore the spiritual part of our beings, we're ignoring a vital part of living.**

The happiest people that I've known live a well-balanced life. They don't just have an emotional, physical, and intellectual balance; they have a *spiritual balance* as well. There is time to develop the spiritual aspect of our lives, if we make it a priority. It's important to set aside at least 15 minutes a day praying or meditating.

Prayer and Meditation: Nourishing Our Spirits.

Since the beginning of recorded history, mankind has worshipped some form of deity. Worship is as fundamental a part of our happiness as anything else discussed in this book. Some people say, "I'm happy and I don't go to church," or "I don't need to go to church," but that's not the point. This is about worshipping and connecting with a higher power in whatever way works for *you*.

It is to our benefit to spend some amount of time every day connecting with God. Connecting with God requires time. For some people that means a structured and very specific way to worship. Whether one prays multiple times a day, or climbs a mountain and finds someplace to meditate, doesn't matter. It isn't important *how* one does it; the important thing is *whether* one does it, consciously and consistently. This is part of how to take care of one's soul. We not only need to eat every morning; our souls need breakfast, too. Meditation, prayer, and scripture reading are a "spiritual breakfast," and that's a great and uplifting way to start off every day.

Wilderness is not a luxury but a necessity of the human spirit.
—**Edward Abbey, Desert Solitaire**

There's something very fulfilling about the quiet solitude of meditation, reaching outside of ourselves and connecting with God. However one defines it, making and maintaining that connection is a vital aspect of happiness. We all need to spend time every day, praying, meditating, or reading the Bible or other spiritual books.

I have always been a spiritual person, but I can't say I consistently and consciously made feeding my spirit a priority until recently. For years, I attended church, prayed, and read from the scriptures, but not consistently. Sometimes my prayers occurred while I was driving in the car, or going for a walk. It was a more informal, less structured way of keeping a spiritual connection to God.

A few years ago when I was facilitating an addiction recovery group, I issued a challenge to the whole group: they were to pray morning and night, on their knees, and to read a few verses from the scriptures each day. I decided to do the same thing in my own life, and it created a stronger, more direct link to God for me. I've experienced a lot of challenges in my life during the past few years. I feel that because of this commitment and the consistent way I've kept it, I've been able to get through those challenges much more easily. Such consistency and structure increases one's ability to hear the "voice of God." Whether one calls it "intuition," "the still, small, voice," the "Spirit," the "Holy Spirit," the "Holy Ghost," or whatever – hearing that voice is a *difference-maker* – it's life changing and a tremendous blessing. The voice of God performs several important functions in our lives: it guides, inspires, soothes, and comforts us.

> *Let us be silent that we may hear the whisper of God.*
> —**Ralph Waldo Emerson**

Once we are in the habit of praying and meditating every day, it's important to remember to listen for an answer. What do we do after saying "Amen" at the end of a prayer? Are we up and "off to the races," or do we stay still and listen? If we meditate after saying our prayers, we'll be listening for an answer. If we ask a question and then don't wait for the answer, we're doing ourselves a disservice, and God, too – then it's only one-sided communication, which really isn't communication. In fact, we need to be tuned in to hear the voice of God at all times, not just at the end of our prayers. In fact, it is entirely possible and actually desirable to stay connected to your higher power throughout your day.

Hearing the Voice of God

> *There is a voice that doesn't use words. Listen!*
> —**Rumi, 13th century Persian poet**

We can't learn to identify and recognize the voice of God unless we spend time in prayer, scripture study and meditation. We need to be very quiet and we have to seek after that voice, to hear it. It takes some effort. We can't pray once and do nothing but hope, then conclude, "Well, I didn't get an answer, forget it! It doesn't work!" *We have to invest time and energy.*

Sometimes hearing the voice of God comes down to simply recognizing it when we hear it. Several years ago, I was speaking publicly and lecturing to youth groups and women's groups on topics like marriage, self-esteem, addiction recovery, and relationships. Time after time, upon finishing a presentation, people approached me and asked if I had written a book, or if I was planning to write a book. After hearing these comments *many times,* I *finally* got it – recognized the message that I should write, and almost immediately, the opportunity opened up. Within 2 weeks I was asked by a large publisher to write a weekly column for one of its newspapers. I was astonished by this unexpected opportunity. When we open ourselves to hear God's voice, then an opportunity to act on it will arise, and it may happen fairly quickly.

Sometimes God may have to be a little more direct to gain our attention if we're not listening. This happened to me several years ago, when I had been working very long hours in my clinical practice. I began to experience severe pains in my stomach. It went on for months; I kept going to the emergency room, and had test after test, yet the doctors weren't able to figure out what was going on. I remember being in my office, doubled over in pain, and asking, "God, why is this happening to me?" I got an immediate answer: "Because you're not listening to me! I'm trying to take you in a different direction."

How many times have you gotten a prompting and you've ignored it? Unfortunately, that's what I had been doing - I ignored the promptings, because I was afraid. I had a thriving practice and I wasn't comfortable dropping that and going in "a different direction." I learned the consequences of ignoring the promptings: your situation gets worse! I had a few more trips to the emergency room, and the terrible stomach pains continued. Finally, in March 2004 I had a major attack in the middle of the day. I was in so much pain, I felt like throwing up; again, I asked, "God, why is this happening to me?" The response I received was immediate and shocking: "If you don't change your ways, I'm going to call you home by the time you're 50." That got my attention! I had little kids, and both of my parents died relatively young. Another prompting came: "I want you to spread the light to a lot more people." I didn't know what that meant, but I was finally listening! I went upstairs and told my wife I had to change my path. It took me the next nine months to slowly exit from my practice; and I didn't regain good health until I had completely changed what I was doing.

Seeing the Hand of God in Our Lives

God is much closer than most of us realize. We need to learn to look for His hand in our lives to recognize His closeness. You may have heard the following story:

> A man was sitting on his porch as floodwaters rose. A woman floated by in a boat, asking if the man needed help. "No, thank you," said the man, "I'm trusting in the Lord." The waters rose higher, sending the man upstairs. A raft full of people floated by his second story window. "Get in," they said, "there's plenty of room." "No thanks," said the man, "I'm trusting in the Lord." The floodwaters kept rising, forcing the man to climb up to the roof. A helicopter swooped in, lowering its ladder for the man. "Thanks anyway," shouted the man, "I'm trusting in the

Lord." Finally, the man was swept away in the torrent and drowned. At the gates of Heaven, the man asked God, "Why didn't you save me?" "What do you mean?" replied God, "I sent two boats and a helicopter!"

—Author unknown

How often in life do we have opportunities like that and not recognize them for what they truly are?

In the end, the number of prayers we say may contribute to our happiness, But the number of prayers we answer may be of even greater importance.
—**Dieter F. Uchtdorf**

We often don't recognize the hand of God, even though it may be very obvious. There is a story about a man who often drank too much. He was running late for a very important meeting with his boss, and he couldn't find a parking space. He drove around the block, desperately searching, until it finally occurred to him to pray for help. "Lord," he pleaded, "if You find me a parking spot, I'll quit drinking." At that moment, a car pulled out in front of him, opening up a parking space. "Never mind," he exclaimed, "**I** found one!" To see the hand of God in our lives, we have to be looking for it.

Develop An Admirable Character Trait

We can nourish our spirits by developing admirable character traits. I am a follower of Jesus Christ. On New Year's Eve of 2010, as I thought about the goals I would pursue and the changes I wanted to make in my life, an interesting thought occurred to me: Which one attribute of Jesus Christ would I most like to emulate, that would have the greatest positive impact in my life? As I pondered this question, I was surprised by how quickly the answer came to me. Out of curiosity, I asked my friends and family the same question. It was astonishing how quickly everyone came up with their own unique answer.

It was impressive that no two people chose the same character trait to work on. A sample of the answers is: "Be more loving," "Be less judgmental," "Be more patient," "Be more forgiving," "Have the courage to stand up for what's right," and "Be more thoughtful of the feelings of others."

If you asked yourself what admirable character trait you would like to adopt, what would your answer be? What attribute of your spiritual leader or God would you choose to develop? By deciding to adopt just one such attribute, you will have the potential to become a little more like that spiritual leader.

Read Good Books

Another way to nourish our spirits is to read good books, including the scriptures, or read from the words of spiritual leaders like the Dalai Lama or the Pope. *The Great Book of Quotes* contains the wisdom of mankind accumulated over thousands of years. All these great books are at our fingertips on the Internet and easily accessed.

Consider all the time that you spend emailing, tweeting, checking out Facebook, etc. There's nothing wrong with that, but if it's all you do, your life is out of balance. If you can spend 4 hours a day reading all the electronic stuff like email, isn't it possible to take 15 minutes to nourish your spirit – to read something that you can incorporate into your life that day?

Temporarily Shut Out the Noise of the World

Although we don't always remember to feed our souls, we continually feed our senses. We live in an overly stimulating world, and it's increasingly more frenetic, every day. All that over-stimulation is the antithesis to spirituality, but there *is* something you can do about it. You just have to make it a habit. When you have a still moment – are stuck in traffic, or sitting in a doctor's office – should you click on your smart phone to check the weather for the 5th time that day – or look at something uplifting for that brief period of time? The noise of all the electronics crowds out the spiritual if we let it; the beauty of technology and the progress man has made is that all information is easily accessible. Even in the middle of the day at work, there's an opportunity to have spiritual balance – instead of checking the news, click on something spiritual and inspirational to read. After all, we do have a choice!

Or even better, remember the media fast that was discussed in Chapter Three? Would you be willing to try that for a day, or even a week?

What are Our Priorities?

If it doesn't matter eternally, does it really matter? We can be emotionally hijacked or upset by things that are really trivial or meaningless when looked at from a long-term perspective. Our time on this earth is so short! Whether we live 20, 50 or 90 years, they fly by. What we *can* do is decide whether we're going to *thrive*

> It's the difference between living and merely existing.

during those years, or just survive. There is a purpose to life, and we all need to figure out what our purpose for being here is.

Finding Our Purpose

People who live with a purpose tend to be happier. When one's life has purpose, it's very different than when one is just aimlessly moving from one day to the next. It's the difference between living and merely existing. During the course of a year or two, several clients recommended that I read *The Purpose Driven Life*, by Rick Warren. The book has sold over 20 million copies, which is absolutely astounding. However, I was busy, didn't have time to read it, and forgot about their recommendations. Then one day I spotted it in Costco and finally bought it.

When I got home, I began reading. The book contains 40 chapters, and the author asks the reader to read one chapter a day, then answer the questions at the end of each chapter (basically the same way I hope you are reading this book.) It's not supposed to be a fast process. Mr. Warren asks the reader to slow down and *really think*. So I was obedient, and did it: I read the whole book in 43 days. It had a big impact on me, helping me through a major transition as I left my private psychology practice and found my second career.

We don't necessarily have to read a book to discover our purpose in life; we all can pray, meditate and take some quiet time to figure out what it is. Finding out God's purpose for your life will bring you happiness. Be open to whatever comes up, rather than trying to dictate the answer. You might be surprised by the results!

Emergency Preparedness for the Soul®

Nobody said life would be easy,
they just promised it would be worth it.
—Harvey Mackay

Let's face it – nobody gets through life unscathed. Those of us who haven't yet faced a major challenge like serious illness, disability, unemployment, or the loss of a loved one, eventually will. If we haven't taken the time to regularly connect with God before one of these challenges strikes, then when a trial does occur, the impact will be much more difficult to take.

I know of a family, one of whose daughters was murdered by her husband when he was in a drunken rage. He had been abusive for the entire term of their short (less than a year) marriage, but she lived in a distant state and none of her family knew about it. This was a large family with a lot of siblings, and their personal faiths ranged from being extremely devoted Christians to not wanting anything to do with religion at all. Fifteen years later, the siblings who embrace the spiritual aspects of their beings have been much better able to deal with their grief, anger and pain. While the loss of their sister still doesn't make sense to them, they've been able to forgive their sister's husband and move on. In contrast, the siblings who have made no effort to develop their spiritual natures continue to suffer greatly with their anger and pain. Their inability to forgive is toxic to their happiness. Having a strong relationship with God and an understanding of the purpose of life will act as a protection to you against the storms of life that will inevitably come. Feeding your spirit is "emergency preparedness for your soul."®

> *Prayer is a lifestyle, not an emergency exit.*
> —Rev. Dr. John E. Manzo

When doctors give a sick person a poor chance of recovery, to whom do most people turn? Even the staunchest of agnostics will usually turn to God. We all need to be in tune with God. Some people really have to stop, pause and listen to recognize His hand in things; for others, it's very obvious. Yet miracles do happen! I've seen so many miracles, I have no doubt that they occur. Doubters may respond to a miracle with attempted explanations such as, "It was a coincidence," or "It was a stroke of good luck," or they may even admit that they can't explain whatever happened. But as a "Believer," I know that miracles do happen. The more we watch, the more we will recognize when miracles occur in our lives.

Have Faith

> *To one who has faith, no explanation is necessary.*
> *To one without faith, no explanation is possible.*
> —Thomas Aquinas

Review your answer to question 25 of the Life Satisfaction Survey you completed for Chapter Two. How did you respond to the statement "I have a strong faith which sustains me throughout my life?" If you responded "Never," or "Rarely," consider whether you will benefit by giving your spirit some nourishment with a strong infusion of faith.

> *Have faith that there is more than you know.*
> *—Hugh Nibley*

Let go and let God carry your burdens. When we have a relationship with God, we don't have to carry our burdens alone. A wonderful poem called "Let Go and Let God" describes this:

Let Go and Let God

As children bring their broken toys with tears for us to mend,
I brought my broken dreams to God because He was my friend.

Instead of leaving Him in peace to work alone . . .
I hung around and tried to help with ways that were my own.

At last I snatched them back and cried, "How can you be so slow?"
"My child," He said, "What could I do? You never did let go . . . "

—Lauretta P. Burns

By having faith in God and allowing Him to help carry our burdens, we relieve ourselves of a terrible load.

The 100 pound backpack. From my experiences working with clients, I learned that most people wake up every morning and before they do anything, they put on what I call their "100 pound backpack," which is filled with their anger, sorrow, anxieties, disappointments, frustrations, and whatever else is troubling them. I think most people don't intentionally or even consciously put it on. But that's how some people walk through life, sometimes for months, years, or even decades. Often we may take a problem to God but not get the answer we want, or as quickly as we'd like. So we take the problem back upon ourselves, and on goes the "100 pound backpack" with the problem stuffed right back inside it. There's great freedom and peace in letting go of our problems and letting God carry them for us. This is where trust and faith in God comes in.

God doesn't give up on us! We may forget God, but He doesn't forget us. Before I was married, I lived in Santa Monica, California. Any apartment in Santa Monica was very expensive, but many of them were under rent control, to allow people who were less affluent (I was a graduate student) to live in a nice area. There was one apartment that I coveted: it was a 2 bedroom, 2 bathroom unit with a big balcony, walking distance from the beach, and on the top floor of the building, for an incredible price. I wanted it so bad, I prayed for it! But I didn't get it, so I forgot about it. Two years later, I ended up getting that exact apartment! As I signed the lease, God's spirit whispered to me, "Well you gave up on it, you stopped praying for it, but I didn't give up on you!" That was our first apartment when Sona and I were married; it's where we lived when our first son was born. It was the last place we lived before we bought our first home. Those years brought us many happy memories.

Faith isn't just a belief; it's an attitude. Several years ago I received an emergency 7:30 a.m. phone call from a client. She was going through some real difficulties because she and her husband were separated; she was raising six kids alone, and working. As we talked, she told me, "My life is not easy, but I feel blessed. I have my kids close to me, we have a roof over our head, and we have enough to eat." She was humble about it. She concentrated on what she had, rather than what she didn't have. She exemplified the power of being grateful, as discussed in Chapter Five, which is one of the great results of having faith in God.

Having faith in God and feeling gratitude, rather than living in fear, can make all the difference in our lives!

Points to Ponder

1. God doesn't give up on us.
2. Let go and let God.
3. With God all things are possible.

Questions to Consider

1. Will you listen for and then act upon the voice of God?
2. Will you look for the hand of God in your life?

Take Action

1. **Pray and Meditate every day.** Pray for 5 minutes every morning: first express your gratitude, then pray for things you need, then listen for 5 minutes: this is your time to receive inspiration, personal revelation, answers to your prayers. Next, read something that's spiritually uplifting for 5 minutes. Whatever you read, put it into practice that day. For example, if you read a scripture about peacemakers, make it a goal and priority to be a peacemaker all day, at home and at work. Implement/act upon the thing you read. This will bless your life and the lives of others. Do this every morning, to start out your day.

Write about your feelings as you're praying or meditating.
_____
_____

How did it affect your day?
_____

2. **Adopt an admirable character trait.**

If you have a religious role model or a spiritual leader, whether it's Jesus Christ, Buddha or the Dalai Lama, look at their attributes: consider which of those attributes you'd like to adopt. Write it down, and start practicing it, every day. Apply it in your life until it becomes one of your own attributes. Then pick another trait and start working on that.

The attribute I'm going to adopt is:
_____
_____

Is adopting this attribute making a difference in my life or in the life of others? If so, how?

_____

3. Read spiritual, uplifting books, including the Bible, on a daily basis.

What are you reading?

_____

What are you learning?

_____
_____

4. "Fast" from media and electronics.

Try eliminating all the electronic over-stimulation in your life for a period of time. Depending on how ambitious you are, try for a day, a week, or longer to live without using the Internet, your cell phone, or having the TV or radio on. If you're serious about doing this, do it for a week or longer. One day isn't enough; even an alcoholic can go a day without alcohol. After a week, you'll really feel it.

This is the reason this chapter is so vitally important to living a balanced life.

How did you feel after a week of no electronics?

_____
_____
_____
_____
_____

5. Daily Spiritual Success Habits Checklist:

Review the following checklist at the end of every day and rank your performance in each area. If you didn't do the task, give yourself a "1." If you did it somewhat, give yourself a "5." A "5" isn't terrible – you still did it, but maybe you didn't apply it. If you did your very best, give yourself a "10".

Daily Checklist: Week of _____	Su	M	T	W	T	F	S
Did I have a heartfelt prayer?							
Did I have meaningful scripture study?							
Did I have an attitude of gratitude?							
Did I keep God in my mind and heart today?							
Did I serve someone else today?							
Was I kind and loving to everyone?							
Was I patient with myself and others?							
Did I spiritually exercise?							
Did I use my time wisely?							

10: I did my best   5: I did it somewhat   1: I didn't do it at all

Chapter Nine

The Sixth Path: Create Loving Relationships

*"Ask not what this relationship can do for you;
Ask what you can do for this relationship!"*

So far, we've talked about different aspects of personal fulfillment and happiness, and most of it has been centered around what we can do for ourselves - focusing on areas in our lives where we can make positive changes. So it might seem like a paradox that to truly find happiness, we also need to focus on what we can do for *others*. Our level of happiness and fulfillment will increase as we improve our relationships with others.

Personal happiness does not exist in isolation; it would actually be a whole lot easier to achieve if it did! From the moment you wake up in the morning, to the moment your head hits the pillow at night, every person with whom you interact is affected by how you see the world, how you see them, and how you see yourself.

Nothing in this life has greater potential to bring us happiness and joy than our relationships. Our memories and experiences with friends and loved ones are the richness of life. Unfortunately, our relationships can also cause us tremendous heartache. The potential for emotional destruction is just as great as is the potential for happiness and joy. Dysfunctional associations can cause us great pain: situations such as a loss of trust, family members not talking to one another, or holding a grudge can affect every aspect of a person's life.

> *Holding a grudge is letting someone live rent-free in your head.*
> —**Unknown**

It makes sense, then, for us to do everything we can to make our relationships with others successful. There are four crucial attributes necessary to have a rewarding connection with another person. We must be 1) loving, 2) understanding, 3) trustworthy, and 4) forgiving. Each of these attributes is multi-faceted.

> *What you leave behind is not what is engraved in stone monuments, but what is woven into the lives of others.*
> – **Pericles**

1. Be Loving

Being loving is obviously the most fundamental building block of a good relationship. But it involves a whole lot more than just having warm feelings toward another person. Love is a verb; it involves *action*.

Furthermore, love is *ongoing* action. Obviously, a husband can't successfully take the position, "I brought you flowers 20 years ago, why are you complaining?!" Love isn't stagnant.

> *Atrophy is the natural process when you stop working a muscle, just as it is if you stop working on your relationship.*
> —**Gerald Rogers**

Love the Other Person in the Way They Need to be Loved. The greatest need human beings have is to feel loved. Each of us has our own, unique way in which we need to feel loved.

The greatest gift we can give another person is to find out how they need to be loved, and then love them in that way. One of my favorite books is *The 5 Love Languages,* by bestselling author Dr. Gary Chapman[1]. In it, Dr. Chapman explains that people express love in five different ways: through words of affirmation, by spending quality time, giving gifts, performing acts of service, and through physical touch (as in holding hands, hugging, and giving back rubs, which is different from sexual touching).

For the first six months of our marriage, my wife Sona and I both believed we were working 110 percent at the relationship. Yet neither of us felt like our needs were being met. It occurred to us one day that we kept having the same disagreement. We talked about how hard we were both working on the marriage, and tried to figure out what was wrong. We both felt frustrated. We finally realized that we each needed to be loved in a different way.

Most likely because of the home in which I grew up, I needed physical touch to feel loved. My family is Greek; my dad adored my mom, and they often expressed physical affection to one another. When I was little, I thought it was cute that my dad would chase my mom around. When I was in high school and he would grab my mom and squeeze her, I didn't think it was quite as cute anymore. One day a friend came home with me and witnessed their affection for one another.

>"Do they do that all the time?" he asked.
>
>"Yes," I muttered, feeling embarrassed and dreading the thought of it being spread all over school.
>
>"That's great!" he exclaimed.
>
>I was shocked! "Excuse me????!!"
>
>And he repeated himself, "That's great! I've *never* seen my parents do that."

That experience completely changed my way of looking at physical affection. After that, I thought it was the way everybody expressed love. So for the first six months of our marriage, that's what I did to express love to my wife. I thought that if I kept doing it, *she'd* start doing it. However, that was not Sona's "love language." Instead, words of appreciation made her feel the most loved. She grew up in a home with parents who were very polite and thanked each other for *everything*, and that was her primary way to express love. I had never before been thanked so many times for everything I did! We were both doing what we hoped the other person would do in return.

As we discussed our frustrations, I told Sona that I was making daily "deposits" into her "love account" – I was always hugging and kissing her. How could she *not* know that I loved her?

"Well, you're putting your deposits into the wrong account," she responded.

I was completely caught off guard to hear that! "You're saying that if I express more appreciation to you, it will be more meaningful than all the hugs and kisses in the world?

"Yes, by far," she confirmed. And then she pointed out, "I tell you 'thank you' all the time. Doesn't that prove how much I love you?"

You can probably guess *my* answer: "Wrong account!"

The change to our marriage took place the very next night when Sona cooked a delicious Greek dinner. I thanked her and complimented her on her cooking. The results were almost magical: she started hugging and kissing me - and I've been saying "thank you" ever since!

Being truly loving, in any relationship, is to love the other person in the way they feel loved. We have to step out of our comfort zones and do something that may not feel natural to us, because it's important to the other person: doing what makes *them* feel loved. That's the most loving, selfless thing we can do.

Love the other person in the way they feel loved.

This principle doesn't only apply to marriage. It applies to *all* of our relationships. For example, we need to recognize our children's "love languages." Some kids need to hear praise; others may need to cuddle a lot. It's neither right nor wrong; it's just the way they are.

On another level, have you ever had a friend who was really great at gift giving? No matter what they picked out, you loved it? That's a person who paid attention to your likes and dislikes. In contrast, I have a friend whose husband used to give her gifts that he would have loved for himself. One year for Mother's Day he gave her a mountain bike! She took one look at the bike and asked him, "Where's yours?" He practically ran out of the room and couldn't get back fast enough with a mountain bike catalog, to show her the one he had picked out for himself! It may have been the easiest thing for him to do in selecting a gift, but it wasn't the best thing he could have done for *her*.

> *Our prime purpose in this life is to help others.*
> *And if you can't help them, at least don't hurt them.*
> —**Dalai Lama**

Refrain From Criticizing. Sometimes it just seems easier to criticize than to praise. We all come from different backgrounds, different family cultures, different perspectives, and often have different ways of doing things. It's all too easy to tell another person that they do something the "wrong" way, instead of praising them for having done it at all. It brings to mind a poem I once heard. It was quoted in a motivational speech given by Lou Holtz, the legendary Notre Dame football coach, author and analyst:

I Watched Them Tear a Building Down

I saw a group of men in my hometown.
I saw a group of men tearing a building down.
With a heave and a ho and mighty yell,
They swung a beam and a side wall fell.
And I said to the foreman, "Are these men skilled,
The type you would hire if you wanted to build?"

Chapter Nine: The Sixth Path: Loving Relationships

And he laughed and said, "Why, no indeed."
He said, "Common labor is all I need.
For I can tear down in a day or two
What it took a builder ten years to do."
And I thought to myself as I walked away,
"Which of these roles am I going to play?
Am I the type that constantly tears down
As I make my way, foolishly around?
Or am I the type that's trying to build with care,
In hope that my loved ones will be glad I was there?"
— Anonymous

I love this poem for its simplicity. It points out the basic question for each of us: "…which role am I going to play?" Will we be builders of our marriages, our families, and our friendships, or will we be wreckers? That's up to each one of us to ponder and decide.

Several years ago a couple came to see me for marital counseling. They were on the verge of divorce after living two decades in a troubled marriage. Their pastor had referred them to me as a last resort. As soon as they walked in, the toxicity level in the room became almost unbearable. Darkness and contention abounded. They sat on opposite ends of the couch with their backs turned to one another. I remember thinking to myself, "This is going to be a LONG hour!"

After asking a lot of questions and getting some of their background information, I asked them if they were ready for their homework assignments. They looked puzzled by my request but reluctantly agreed. My philosophy has always been that by giving "homework" and holding people accountable, it will become obvious who really wants to change and who's just "going through the motions." Healing a relationship only works when the individuals involved are both willing to make a concerted effort, and I wouldn't want anyone to be wasting their money, or my time, for that matter.

I turned to the husband first and said, "If you could ask your wife to do ONE thing for you during the next week, what would it be?" He immediately responded, "I would like for her to stop threatening me with divorce every day when I walk in the house after work! I'm sick and tired of hearing that threat and can't stand it anymore!" I turned to the wife and asked her if she would comply, and she unenthusiastically nodded "yes". "Great!" I exclaimed. "After the week is over, you can go right back to threatening him with divorce again!" I was kidding, of course, but at least I was able to get her to smile.

I then asked the wife if there was one thing that she would like her husband to do for her over the next seven days, at which point she started to cry. I waited in silence for a minute and repeated the question. She finally replied, "I wish he would stop criticizing me for a week." That seemed like a very reasonable request, so I turned to him to get his approval. But to my astonishment, his answer was, "Well, I don't know if I can do that!"

I quickly rejoined, "Listen, your wife just promised not to threaten you with divorce and all she's asking in return is not to be criticized for one week. I don't care what you have to do: go for a walk with the dog, go for a drive, go to your room and close the door; or if you have no other options, bite your tongue 'til it bleeds. But you may NOT criticize her for a week. Is that clear???" He finally acquiesced, but it was obviously under duress. I also asked him to keep an accounting of how often he felt like criticizing her; I wanted to get an actual number to find out how prevalent this behavior was. He agreed to do both, and they left.

I saw them exactly one week later and as was customary, I initially visited with them one at a time. When I went to the waiting room, I asked to see the wife first …. but I honestly didn't recognize her. I'm not sure what had transpired during the week, but the dark circles under her eyes were gone. As a matter of fact, her entire countenance was different. I asked her if she had kept her promise not to threaten her husband with divorce, to which she replied in the affirmative. I then asked how her husband had done with his promise. She started to sob, but was eventually able to tell me that this was the first week since they had gotten married 21 years ago in which she had not been criticized by him. It was as though a huge burden had been lifted from her. It was no wonder she looked so much better.

Next, I asked to see the husband and asked him the same questions. He also said it had been one of the better weeks they had had as a couple in a very long time. Coming home every evening and not hearing the word "divorce" had made things easier. I then inquired, "How did it go with your promise?" He told me completely straight-faced that it was the hardest thing anyone had ever asked him to do! I assumed he was exaggerating, until he told me how many times he had felt like criticizing his wife that week: an astounding 280 times! To this day, that number remains the all-time record of anyone with whom I've worked!

I sat with this husband and broke that number down to give him some perspective. We determined the following: 280 weekly criticisms, divided by 7 days equals about 40 per day on the average. If he slept 8 hours and went to work for 10 (including commuting time), that left 6 hours a day. Taking a couple more hours off during which time the wife drove their kids to activities, there were approximately four hours left in each day when the two of them were together. "Do you realize," I asked him, "that amounts to 10 criticisms per hour, or 1 every 6 minutes?" The severity of the problem had never dawned on him, until that moment.

I asked both of them to commit to their promises for another week... and then another, and another. Slowly and with a lot of work, this couple that was on the verge of divorce was able to not only save their marriage, they created a loving home. They truly progressed from *barely* surviving to thriving! Of course they were not perfect, but by changing just one behavior each, they were able to eliminate huge emotional "withdrawals" from their marriage and move back from the verge of "marital bankruptcy" to rebuilding their "trust accounts." Obviously not all examples are this dramatic, but criticism can and does take a huge toll on any relationship.

> **Criticism can and does take a huge toll on any relationship.**

Kind words can be short and easy to speak, but their echoes are truly endless.
—**Mother Teresa**

Be Complimentary: The Power of a Compliment. Paying somebody a compliment really doesn't cost anything. But what's the benefit of it? One kind word can change another person's day, or even their entire life. It's important that compliments be sincere, and specific. This is not about flattering someone, but rather genuinely sharing an insight or observation that comes from your heart. It will make them feel good about themselves. It's part of loving people, and having good relationships. I would urge you to find at least one person every day to compliment. See how it makes *you* feel to make someone else's day better.

Constructive Criticism is an Oxymoron. Nothing good, healthy or positive comes from being criticized. Parenting experts have repeatedly stated that for every negative or critical comment directed towards a child, it takes ten positive comments to counteract its impact. That's right -TEN!! Some people argue that if a comment is "constructive" and the criticism is well-intended, then that's ok, but I've learned otherwise from my own experience.

I remember once criticizing my youngest son and justifying it in my mind thinking, "It's for his own good. . . I'm only saying this to him so he can do better next time." But after I made the comment, I felt terrible, and my son felt worse about himself. What part of that exchange was constructive? Consider it from your own perspective: have you ever changed a behavior because you were criticized "enough?"

> *Have you ever changed a behavior because you were criticized "enough?"*

> *People never change because they are under threat or under duress. Never. They change because they see something that makes their life seem valuable enough to start moving toward a life worth living.*
> —Robert Downey, Jr.

Be Respectful. Another important way to express our love for others is to be respectful to them. Every person deserves respect, simply by virtue of the fact that they are a human being, and therefore of great worth - even if we don't approve of the way that person is acting.

> ***Respect is an expression of our sense of universal brotherhood or sisterhood—a testimony of our membership in the human family.***
> ***—Gary Chapman***

Respect should be a part of every communication and every action, even if it's just a fleeting, one-time encounter with somebody like the drive-up person at a fast food restaurant. There are many ways of being respectful, but it includes being polite, kind, using a gentle tone of voice, showing empathy, concern, caring, and deferring to appropriate boundaries that have been set by others. Prejudice and gossiping are both disrespectful behaviors that demean others. And it's never okay to justify being disrespectful to another person because they've done something to wrong us – that's shifting responsibility for our behavior to the other person.

Before You Speak . . . Think!

T – is it True?
H – is it Helpful?
I – is it Inspiring?
N – is it Necessary?
K – is it Kind?

—Bob Lenz

It's just as important for parents to show their children respect, as it is for children to be respectful of their parents. We generally *demand* respect from our kids – but do *we* respect *them?* The best way to get respect isn't to demand it – it's to extend respect, to teach by our example.

I once worked with a 14-year-old girl who had been sent by her parents for counseling because she was engaging in some risky behaviors, and they were worried that she was spiraling out of control. As we talked during the first session, she told me, "I just need my space to try to figure things out, so I can make better choices. I'm not doing anything bad now; I realize I made mistakes, I was stupid." She had learned from her mistakes and wanted to get on a better path. But her parents had grounded her indefinitely from everything; they took her phone away, took away all of her privileges, and following that, her grades had gone way down. The parents were justifiably concerned, but their overreaction seemed to exacerbate the problem more, instead of solving it. The daughter no longer felt like she mattered; she no longer felt respected.

I reminded the parents that she was a good kid; she just had made some poor choices. When they believed in her and gave her "a little space," she turned her life around. I've parented teenagers and I know this isn't easy, but sometimes we have to show our kids we have faith in them, or they won't have faith in themselves. We still have to make sure they're safe and have boundaries, but they need a little room, too. Nobody likes to be boxed in completely!

How many times have you been in a grocery store and cringed when you witnessed an overwhelmed parent loudly berating a child over some small infraction, or worse, physically abusing them? You've also probably noticed that children don't respond positively to that kind of treatment. Nobody does!

Interestingly, people who have *self-respect* tend to treat others with respect. They don't feel like they have to put other people down to make themselves feel good. It all basically comes down to "the golden rule:" **We need to treat other people the way *we* want to be treated.**

Allow Other People to Be Themselves – Don't Try to Control Them.
There's *nothing* loving about trying to control another human being; in fact, it's the opposite of being loving. It happens in relationships all the time; I've seen countless examples of it when doing marriage counseling. Trying to control the behavior of another is not being accepting of the other person. Nor does it have positive results. Typically the byproduct of trying to control another is resentment. You might get what you want if they fear you, but it will not engender feelings of love for you. And the first opportunity they have to get out of the relationship, they will.

> Trying to control the behavior of another is not being accepting of the other person.

Many years ago, I received a phone call from a distraught woman who wanted to see me right away. She had just met with her minister, seeking his support for ending a marriage of just a few months. I had several questions about her impending decision. She told me her story and the reason(s) for making such a seemingly quick and rash decision. Even though she had only been married a short time, her family was having a hard time physically recognizing her. Her self-esteem had plummeted so dramatically that they were actually concerned for her well-being.

She had married a man who on the outside and during the courtship had shown nothing that would arouse any suspicions of his controlling nature. All was well until the day of the wedding…and then it started. First was a suggestion that she would look better if she changed her hair. Then on the honeymoon, she was pressured to wear revealing clothes she was not comfortable wearing. After the honeymoon, the control shifted to how she should fold clothes, or how much soap needed to go into the dishwasher, etc. Slowly, a lovely young woman who had previously had great self-esteem was being reduced to one with very little self-worth. Any attempts to find a compromise were met with increased anger and more attempts to control her. Any suggestions of going to their minister or seeking a counselor were quickly dismissed with, "I don't have any problems; you do."

After listening carefully for an hour, I finally asked her: "Why now?" I wanted to know what had prompted her to take such an action at this time. She told me that much prayer and meditation had led her to the realization of what would happen if she brought kids into such an environment. If she had sons, they would learn to treat women the same way their father was treating her: with control, domination and a total lack of respect. If she had daughters, they would grow up thinking that they didn't deserve any better. This story actually had a happy ending. She divorced her first husband and soon married a wonderful, loving, kind and compassionate man who loved her for *who she was*.

To provide some psychological perspective on the issue, most people who are controlling have had something happen in their life that was either painful or felt so out of their control, they vowed never to be in such a position again. **Only an insecure person seeks to control another and rob them of their free will!** Whether it's done consciously or unconsciously is not as important as their ability to acknowledge it. It's ironic that most people who are controlling used to themselves feel out of control, and in their attempt to protect themselves, they became the very thing to which they objected in the beginning.

Be Selfless. The root of most dysfunctional relationships is selfishness. People who approach a friendship, romance or marriage with the philosophy of "What's in it for me? What can I get out of this relationship?"

are not looking to love or care for the other person. This kind of an approach creates unhappy, unhealthy and even abusive relationships. Almost all negative behaviors or thoughts arise from selfishness.

The mind-set of people in relationships that thrive is quite different. Their approach is more "How can I make the other person's life better? How can I be a better husband/wife/friend/parent?" One of my favorite quotes comes from President John F. Kennedy's 1961 Inaugural Address, when he said, ". . . Ask not what your country can do for you - ask what you can do for your country."

Consider if the word "country" was replaced with "marriage" or "friendship" or "relationship." What can you do for your husband or wife? For your son or daughter? For your mother or father? For your friend? *That's* the correct way to build loving, thriving, healthy and uplifting relationships. In the course of marital counseling, I often suggest to clients that they should "Ask not what this relationship can do for you — ask what you can do for this relationship." **That is the formula for any successful relationship.**

> **Almost all negative behaviors or thoughts arise from selfishness.**

Tell People You Care About Them! If we don't tell the people we care about how we truly feel, they may never know. The following experience was told by John Powell in his book, *The Secret of Staying in Love:*

> It was the day my father died . . . . In the small hospital room, I was supporting him in my arms, when . . . my father slumped back, and I lowered his head gently onto the pillow.

I . . . told my mother . . . "It's all over, Mom. Dad is dead."

She startled me. I will never know why these were her first words to me after his death. My mother said: "Oh, he was so proud of you. He loved you so much."

Somehow I knew . . . that these words were saying something very important to me. They were like a sudden shaft of light, like a startling thought I had never before absorbed. Yet there was a definite edge of pain, as though I were going to know my father better in death than I had ever known him in life.

Later, while a doctor was verifying death, I was leaning against the wall in the far corner of the room, crying softly. A nurse came over to me and put a comforting arm around me. I couldn't talk through my tears. I wanted to tell her:

"I'm not crying because my father is dead. I'm crying because my father never told me that he was proud of me. He never told me that he loved me. Of course, I was expected to know these things. I was expected to know the great part I played in his life and the great part I occupied of his heart, but he never told me."[2]

2. Be Understanding

> *Be kind, for everyone you meet is fighting a hard battle.*
> — **Plato**

After feeling loved, the second greatest need that people have is to feel understood. Have you ever spent time with someone, and as you parted, thought to yourself, "Wow, he/she totally gets me"? It feels so wonderful – almost like coming home – recognizing that someone understands us, instead of judges us. It's a priceless thing that we can offer other people. On the other hand, if we're confiding in somebody and feel like they're critical of us, or trying to solve a problem we don't really want them to solve, we don't feel loved. When we think, "that person doesn't *get* me," it causes unhappiness or frustration in the relationship.

Most of us have experienced a reunion with a friend we haven't seen for a long time, and discovered that we are able to pick up right where we left off. It's as though there was never any separation. The reason for that is because we have a connection with that person. No matter the distance or time, we give them a hug and it's just like we saw them yesterday.

So what creates that kind of a connection? It's the byproduct of having consistent, positive, empathetic, and loving encounters with that person over time. That way, when we see them again, the first association is a warm feeling. It would be incredible to have that kind of a deep and profound connection with all of our friends and loved ones, whether we talk to them every day, or only see them every 10 years at some kind of reunion.

It works the same way in the reverse. If we have a negative interaction with somebody, what's the first thing we think the next time we see them? "I want to give them a hug?" Not likely! From the outset, you're going to try to read how they're reacting. And if you have more than one negative interaction with that person, before long you're not going to want to have any interactions with them.

Communication. We each go to great lengths to make sure we can express ourselves in a way that others will understand us. There is something very comforting in knowing we are not alone in our way of thinking, feeling or viewing life. Communication therefore becomes the vehicle by which most of us attempt to really connect with one another. Marvin J. Ashton once said,

"If we would know true love and understanding one for another, we must realize that communication is more than a sharing of words. It is the wise sharing of emotions, feelings, and concerns. It is the sharing of oneself totally."[3]

The following are four important components of effective communication:

1) Active and Authentic Listening

The most important part of communication is listening. It's an act of love to be able to listen to somebody. Truly listening is more than just being silent. It's giving undivided attention when somebody else needs to be heard. When we listen with a "third ear," which is listening with our hearts - active and authentic listening – we get the substance, the meaning behind the words, of what people are trying to communicate to us. *Then* we can understand what's going on.

Following is an amusing story about a husband who wanted to make his wife's birthday the best day possible:

> Several days prior to her big day he asked her what she wanted for her birthday. Without hesitation she answered him, "I would love to be 6 again!" The husband immediately began to plan a day she would never forget. On

the morning of her birthday she woke up to breakfast in bed. The only other day of the year she normally had such a treat was on Mother's Day. This however, was not your typical breakfast…It included chocolate milk, cereal and two fresh, warm donuts. Although surprised by this culinary feast, she indulged her husband. As soon as she was finished, he whisked her off to the local amusement park. He took her on every ride imaginable: the screaming upside down giant rollercoaster, the Temple of Destruction, the Tower of Doom etc. A couple of hours later she stumbled out of the park, a little queasy from all the rides, especially after that very "healthy" breakfast she had started with.

But her good husband was not done yet. He took her to one of her favorite fast food places and ordered the extra value meal with a ton of French-fries and a big chocolate shake! He then took her to the latest Star Wars epic, bought her the refillable tub of popcorn and her favorite candy. When they finally got home, she collapsed on her bed exhausted and a little sick from the day's events. At last the proud husband walked up to her with a big smile on his face and said to his dear wife, "Well honey, what was it like being 6 again?" After a few bewildered moments, an understanding and realization finally dawned in her eyes, and she blurted out, "I meant my dress size, you idiot!!!"

There was a communication problem, but this husband was surely trying to show his wife that he loved her.

I remember how the communication issue played out when my wife and I were first married. I thought I could take a few shortcuts and still qualify as having listened to her. For example, sometimes Sona cooked dinner in the kitchen and talked to me while I was watching sports on the TV in the adjoining room. I soon discovered that there were some key phrases I could use while watching my games that would give the impression that I was really listening to my wife, (phrases such as, "Sounds great honey. . ." or "Whatever you say dear…") Of course, it wasn't long before she caught on to the fact that I was not seriously paying attention to what she was saying, and one day she did the unthinkable: she stepped in front of the TV and turned it off during the 4th quarter of a game! To say the least, I was incredulous and demanded, "What are you doing?" She calmly replied, "You're not really listening to me, are you?" To which I responded, "Of course I am." Then she asked a question that threw me for a moment: "Do you know what you just agreed to do?" I was totally clueless, so I tried stalling for time, but it was too late - I was caught red-handed! She told me that I had just agreed to cook dinner for ten people on Sunday! It was humiliating to have been exposed like that. So I vowed from that day forward, whenever my wife talked to me, I would actively listen to her.

When you talk, you are only repeating what you already know, but when you listen, you may learn something new.
— **Dalai Lama**

It's hard work to listen attentively to another person if it isn't a habit for you. **It takes time, patience, and selflessness.** Many people love to talk about themselves! Have you ever spent time with somebody whose opening is, "How are you? But anyway, enough about you! Let me tell you about the incredible thing I did last week!" How much fun is that to be around?

A friend of mine had known another couple for about 15 years. She and her husband occasionally went out to dinner with them, and she always dreaded it when her husband and the other wife became engaged in a conversation and abandoned her to talk with the other man. He went on so much about himself, one night she found herself wondering, "Do you even know my name?!" If she tried to tell him about anything that had been going on in her life, he immediately turned the conversation back to himself, without much recognition of what she had said. She eventually told her husband that dates with that couple were not much fun, and they stopped going out with them. Effective communication is an mutual exchange of information and feelings.

2) Differences of Opinion

Effective communication is an exchange of information and feelings.

It's almost impossible not to occasionally experience differences of opinion in a relationship, no matter how good the connection between two people may be. It seems to be a natural reaction for us to try to convince the other person that they should see things the way *we* do. The selfish part of us likes to explain ourselves and our position first. The more loving part of ourselves, however, first listens to the other party's perspective. Differences shouldn't be a point of contention; rather, they should be weighed and evaluated calmly. **What's more important, convincing the other person that your point or opinion is correct, or having a healthy, continuing conversation?** We may even find ourselves learning something from the other person when we try to understand their position. At the very least, we will learn more about how they think and feel – about who they really are. When we meet with an open heart and mind, the outcome of a discussion can't help but be a success. Active and authentic listening becomes an extension of expressing the fact that we care.

> *10% of conflicts are due to difference in opinion,*
> *90% is due to wrong tone of voice.*
> —**Ritu Ghatourey**

3) Refrain From Passing Judgment

Active and authentic listening also means we need to avoid judging the person who is speaking. If we are truly trying to understand, we won't be critical. Showing disgust or shock in regard to another's comments is not conducive to good communication, nor is it respectful. We shouldn't impose our values on another person. If someone we care about is making a bad decision, we can convey the attitude that we don't agree, but it's important to also make it clear that we respect their right to decide, and that we still care about them.

If we disagree with what a friend or loved one is saying, our focus shouldn't be on "What's *wrong* with him/her," but instead on what's *good* about him/her. Looking for the good in somebody helps us feel better about them if we have a disagreement, and we might realize that they may be disagreeing because they're trying to help us, rather than disagreeing because they're trying to point out that they're smarter than we are. Too often people use periods of communication to dictate to or threaten the other person. **In a loving relationship, communication**

should never be used to command or embarrass another. Only kind and thoughtful words are appropriate. If negative feelings need to be expressed, it should be done in a respectful manner using "I" messages, not "you" (blaming or critical) messages.

4) Embrace Differences

It's important to recognize that you and the other person in a relationship are different, but those differences can *complement* one another. Value the strengths the other person brings to the relationship that might be weaknesses for you. Learn to focus on the other person's good characteristics, and praise them.

None of us is perfect, but if we feel accepted unconditionally, we will feel loved. Likewise, we should accept others unconditionally. Far too often, women find themselves battling with an issue of self-acceptance. This, coupled with a perceived or real lack of acceptance by their spouse, can give their self-worth a beating. This is one of the root causes of depression which far too often plagues women. Imagine a relationship where mistakes, imperfections, weaknesses, (as well as gifts, talents and strengths) are accepted without judgment. In that scenario, a person couldn't help but feel loved.

> **If we feel accepted unconditionally, we will feel loved.**

3. Be Trustworthy

The third critical element and cornerstone of any successful relationship is trust. Whether we're talking about friendship, family, or workplace relationships, it all comes down to trust. Have you ever been in a relationship that was wrecked because of a breach of trust? I used to believe that all a person needed in a relationship was love. Over the years, I've learned that many previously loving relationships came to a crashing halt when trust was severely violated. I've known many couples that have loved each other deeply but could not overcome repeated "withdrawals" from the "trust account" in their marriage. The love may still have been there, but the lack of trust made a continued relationship almost impossible. Breaches of trust come in a variety of ways: most common are outright lies, such as when a parent asks a child, "Did you brush your teeth?" The child answers, "Yes," but the toothbrush isn't even wet when the parent checks it. That's pretty straightforward. Trust is also violated when we make a promise to someone but then either don't follow through - or even worse - choose to do the exact opposite. An example of that is when an addict "swears" they're quitting the substance they're addicted to for the 50th time. All they're asking for is another chance. Although the desire might be sincere, the credibility factor is down to zero: too many broken promises. Integrity is the first casualty of an addict. It's the first thing to get lost, because to maintain their secret life, they have to lie. It's the reason a relationship with an addict is so painful – they can't be trusted.

There are some actions that can empty the "trust" account in a relationship overnight. The big three are infidelity, addictions, and abuse of any kind. They each strike at the heart of the relationship.

Another big breach of trust is a failure to keep confidences. A friend of mine once told her husband a colorful story about her sister's past in confidence. A few days later, while he was on a business trip, he unintentionally called home from his cell phone (some people call this "butt-dialing!") Unbeknownst to him, his wife listened in as he regaled a business colleague with the story about her sister – it was just too juicy for him to keep to himself. The breach of confidence was tremendously hurtful to his wife, and it made a major withdrawal from the "trust account" of their marriage.

Regaining Trust. Can someone regain trust once it has been lost? The answer is an absolute YES, but with certain stipulations. The following are three steps necessary to repair a relationship that has been damaged because of a breach of trust:

1) Make a Conscious Decision to be Truthful

To rebuild trust in a relationship, the offending party needs to make a conscious decision to be truthful, no matter what the consequences are. Parents try to teach this concept to their children on a daily basis, especially by example. I heard a story about a mother who found a way to make a strong impression upon her 4-year-old son about the consequences of lying. For weeks this little boy had told lie after lie, and despite his mother's repeated lectures that it was wrong to lie, he continued. Finally, one day when they were running errands, the mother told her son that if he behaved well, she'd take him to get ice cream when the errands were done. Boy, was he excited! He was as good as gold – and therefore quite shocked when his mother drove right past the ice cream store without stopping on their way home.

> "Mom!" he exclaimed. "You didn't stop at the ice cream store!"
>
> Driving on, she looked at him over her shoulder, smiled and responded, "I lied!"

There was no trip to get ice cream that day, and that little boy was cured pretty quickly of lying.

I believe that the consequences for lying should be more severe than the consequences for the wrongful act that the lie covered up. When someone is used to lying, it is not easy to lose the habit. Just like in the case of a recovering addict, it's not only one day at a time, but one decision at a time that is critical: to lie, or to tell the truth? That one question will determine to a large degree the success or failure of any relationship.

2) Become a "Promise Keeper!"

Wouldn't our society be better if we all kept our promises? The impact of just following through with our promises would transform all of our relationships. Think of the implications of saying something and then actually following through! Not only would trust be re-established, but relationships would thrive.

I discovered the benefit of this principle in my own life when I decided that I needed to start keeping my promises, even the little ones. It began with my interactions with my youngest son, Dmitri. I was inspired to make a change because I was afraid I was going to damage my relationship with him. He was only 5 years old, and he'd often come into my office and ask me if I'd play basketball with him. My response was always the same: "I'm busy with 'important stuff;' come back in half an hour." He had barely learned how to read a clock, and yet he'd be back in 29 minutes and 58 seconds, so excited to play with his dad. But I was still too busy, and as I sent him away again, he left with a disappointed look on his face. Over a period of a few weeks, the third or fourth time this happened, a voice in my head said, "If you keep doing this, he'll stop asking." It was like somebody had thrown a bucket of cold water in my face.

"What are you *doing?!*" I asked myself. I had a client on the phone with me at that moment, but I realized my son was more important. I had already spent the designated hour with the client. So I ended the phone call, and went outside and played basketball with Dmitri. He only wanted 15 or 20 minutes of my time. It had been painful to see the hurt I caused because I didn't keep my promises to him. And so I adopted a new guideline for myself that year: to keep my promises, even the little ones. As a result, I became more responsible and more accountable. Even more importantly, I was no longer disappointing my son. If a person keeps their promises to the people they love, what a difference that will make in their life! The change I made had a positive effect on *all* of my relationships, including my work relationships.

3) Consistency is Key to Success.

Far too often, we see someone violate another's trust and then expect that by being "good" for a short time, they should have all of their privileges restored. This is especially true in the case of teenagers, or those who have the emotional maturity of a teenager. Passive passage of time is not enough, but **a consistent and proactive approach will do wonders.** Seek to find opportunities to rebuild trust and at the same time, remember to manage your expectations. If there's a true change of heart, a person won't give up being honest just because the rewards take a long time to arrive. Otherwise, they're just trying to get back into the good graces of the one they've offended, not really experiencing a change of heart. Basically, they're just trying to pacify their loved one so they don't have to pay the consequences. It has some short-term benefits, but long-term, it's even more devastating. Because it results in another betrayal, even bigger: they're just "behaving" to buy themselves some time, to take the pressure off.

4. Be Forgiving

Being forgiving is the fourth crucial attribute necessary to have a rewarding connection with another person. For a relationship to be truly healed, forgiveness has to be sought by the offender and extended by the offended. Since none of us are perfect and we all make mistakes, forgiveness is a necessity for any relationship to thrive.

When someone has offended us, the crucial question is, what do we do with that hurt? Do we build walls around ourselves? Or in spite of the pain, do we decide, "Just because I got hurt by this person, it doesn't mean everybody's like that?" Our faith in other people needs to continue regardless of what has happened in previous relationships.

> Making amends is one of the most loving things we can do in a relationship.

Be Responsible and Make Amends. When we are the offending party, we need to take responsibility and make amends for any hurt or damage that we have caused to a relationship. Taking responsibility is hard for some people to do because of pride, but it's crucial to healing a rift. Interestingly, the more we do it, the easier it becomes. Making amends is one of the most loving things we can do in a relationship. It goes far beyond saying "I'm sorry." It's taking action, not just giving "lip service." I don't mean to minimize the importance of an apology, but if we truly want to mend a broken relationship, we need to put more effort into it. Obviously, the bigger the "offense" was, the more important it is for us to make amends.

A word of caution: We cannot continue to ask for forgiveness and then revert to old habits. We need to apply the other three steps for repairing a relationship consistently and diligently — that's what a sincere change of heart looks like! The peace of mind that comes with consistently telling the truth and keeping promises is invaluable, and certainly much better than the short-term "reward" of temporarily getting away with dishonesty.

> *I've learned that people will forget what you said, people will forget what you did,*
> *But people will never forget how you made them feel.*
> —Maya Angelou

Toxic Relationships

As important as it is to have thriving, loving and connected relationships, it's equally important to eliminate or at least set boundaries on any toxic relationships in your life. This is a *key ingredient* to your personal happiness, because even one disastrous relationship can hijack your peace of mind and well-being. If your child came home crying every time after they played with a bully, would you send them back to play with the kid? Of course not! You'd want to protect them and cut off the bully. In the same way, you need to protect *yourself* from toxic relationships.

We cannot continue to ask for forgiveness and then revert to old habits.

Have you ever walked by a recently fertilized lawn or a wastewater treatment plant that stinks to high heavens? Do you just keep standing there, and take more breaths, or do you leave?" It's the same with relationships; why continue to be around somebody that creates damage? While the bad odor of sewage only damages one's sense of smell, a toxic relationship damages one's sense of worth. It's far more toxic. One is temporary - a person can walk 100 yards away and no longer smell it -

but damage from a toxic relationship can stay in your soul for decades. Do you want to smell the sewage for decades?

Identifying a Toxic Relationship. How do we identify the toxic relationships in our lives? In a healthy relationship, we feel connected, fulfilled, listened to, energized, uplifted and loved. The more relationships we have where we feel this way, the happier our lives will be. In contrast, a toxic relationship is based on negativity, criticism, addiction, or emotional, verbal or physical abuse. Feelings of unworthiness and low self-esteem are quite common in people who are exposed long-term to someone who is toxic for them. Often it is someone who is significant in his/her life: a spouse, parent, child, sibling, a colleague at work or a so-called "friend." These relationships are typically co-dependent, controlling, dysfunctional and destructive.

Sometimes it's necessary to take a step back and assess the situation. What are you really getting out of this relationship? It can be helpful to ask the following questions:

- How do I *consistently* feel after I've had an interaction with this individual?
- Do I feel down on myself?
- Do I feel stressed, fearful and anxious?
- Do I feel drained of energy and devoid of good feelings?
- Do I feel resentful?

If the answer is "yes" to most of these questions, then certainly you are involved in a toxic relationship. This is not the same as getting into an argument with someone you love, because that happens to everybody once in a while, and those feelings will also likely come up. But if negative feelings are the *usual* pattern you have in most of your interactions with that person, then it qualifies as a toxic relationship. There are four red flags that can also help to identify a toxic relationship:

1. The other person is selfish or prideful; or
2. They are controlling; or
3. They constantly criticize you; or
4. There is an absence of forgiveness if you've made a mistake (or if *they think* you've done something wrong).

> *You cannot hang out with negative people and expect to live a positive life.*
> —**Joel Osteen**

How Do We Deal With Toxic Relationships? We need to differentiate between people we can cut out of our lives once and for all, and those we can't so easily, such as family members. If we have a toxic relationship with one of our siblings, one of our kids, or even a parent, it's much more complicated to "divorce" them from our lives. We can stop talking to them or stop having meaningful interactions, but they are still family. Does this mean we need to endlessly endure their toxicity? <u>Absolutely not!</u> We have every right to limit, if not altogether eliminate, negative interactions with them. We have the right to minimize the amount of contact we have with them.

The responsibility to protect ourselves lies within each of us, and it is best achieved by setting healthy boundaries. They are the key to eliminating or minimizing the impact of unhealthy relationships. Most people, however, do not know *how* to set healthy boundaries and often question themselves if they are being rude for doing so. Yet the rules of kindness and civility apply to *everyone,* including our families. **Just because someone is part of our family doesn't give him or her the freedom to be rude or mean.**

There are several ways to set healthy boundaries. One is to make any contact with the toxic person very superficial. It's a conscious decision not to share anything personal with them, if every time we do, the person ends up hurting us.

Another healthy boundary is to set time limits. If you can only take your father-in-law for two hours, and then he drives you crazy, limit your visit to an hour and a half. For example, have an appointment at the end of the visit, so you have to leave. That will also give you a sense of control. Setting time limits are also helpful in situations where family functions are difficult. Stay less, rather than overstaying, even if things are going well. It's always preferable to have an outcome of "Oh, we didn't get to spend enough time with you" rather than, "I can't believe they stayed so long!"

At some point it may be necessary to have a very frank discussion with a toxic family member, to lay out for them the boundaries you have set. For example, suppose someone in your extended family, like your mother, is constantly being critical of you and your skills as a parent and then wonders why you avoid spending time with her. The best way to handle this situation — and it takes a lot of courage — is to say something along the following lines in a calm and direct manner:

> "Mom, growing up in our home I was on the receiving end of a lot of criticisms from you. When I got married and we decided to have a family, my husband/wife and I made a vow that we would raise our children in an envi-

ronment of love, acceptance and forgiveness. There will be no daily criticisms of them regardless of what they do. Next time you come and visit, I expect that if you have anything negative to say to my kids or me you will keep it to yourself. If you don't respect my wishes, your visit will be short-lived. I will ask you to leave. I'd like to have a relationship with you, and I hope you can enjoy your grandchildren for a long time, but this is my bottom line. I don't want to raise my kids around the same toxicity that I was raised with. Will you respect my wishes?"

If she says anything but a definite "yes" then you respond by saying, "Well, I guess we won't be spending a lot of time with you, then." It only takes a couple of times of enforcing healthy boundaries before people's behaviors change for the better, or the relationship becomes superficial and limited. Interestingly, when there are clearly defined boundaries, parameters and consequences, most people respect them. They behave because they know what the cost will be if they don't. You're not being a mean son or daughter – you're just saying, "that's unacceptable behavior in *my* home." It's very empowering to set healthy boundaries.

This approach also works really well with friends, except that we have more leeway. Life is way too short to keep "friends" who are toxic. Our lives are so busy that we hardly have enough time to spend with friends who give back in a positive way.

You may want to take inventory of the relationships in your life and see if any of them fall into the toxic category. If any of them do, then hopefully you will have the inner strength to do something about it. Creating healthy boundaries is a gift to yourself that will pay great dividends for years to come.

Tact is the ability to tell someone to go to hell in such a way that they look forward to the trip.
—**Winston Churchill**

Points to Ponder:

1. Relationships: They're all about love!
2. If you want to be happy, there is no room for toxic relationships in your life.
3. Love the other person in the way they need to be loved.

Questions to Consider:

1. Are you a promise-keeper?
2. Are you an active listener?
3. Has criticism ever changed you?

Take Action

1. If you were to take an accounting of all your vital relationships, after what you've just read, are they thriving? Are they emotional "paychecks"? Or are they negative and destructive? Make a list of parents, siblings, kids, relatives and friends, and do a little mini-survey with a rating scale of 1-10 for each of them. A "10" means the relationship is thriving, a "5" is doing okay (they don't detract from us, but they may not add that much, either), and a rating of "1, 2 or 3" means the relationship is toxic and dysfunctional. It's time to identify toxic relationships and decide what you want to do with them. Will you cut them off? Or move them into the "middle zone," make them more tolerable?

My relationships: Rating:

1. _____
2. _____
3. _____
4. _____
5. _____
6. _____
7. _____
8. _____
9. _____
10. _____

2. Consider the relationships you rated as a "5" or less. Are these relationships worth preserving, or do you need to remove them from your life? Typically, a relationship that would get rated as a "5" is okay, it doesn't add a lot to your life, and it takes work, but it is tolerable. Contemplate why you are holding on to such relationships. Either make changes that will improve the relationship's rating, or get rid of it. If you have relationships in your life that you rated a "3", "2", or "1", the question to ask yourself is, "Why do I have them in my life? They are detracting from my happiness. They are toxic to me." Review the section of Chapter Nine that discusses Toxic Relationships as you evaluate each relationship you rated a "4" or less, and with that specific person in mind, ask yourself: "What am I willing to do about this?" If your response is "nothing," you need to realize that it takes away from your overall happiness. "Nothing" is not the right answer! You either cut that person out of your life or improve the relationship to at least a "5" or a "6," to make it tolerable. **Remember, the best use of this book is as a call to action in order for you to be happier in your life**

3. Consider a relationship you feel is in jeopardy —not bad, but not great— yet you don't want to downgrade it to a "toxic" rating because you want to save it. Remember that asking for that person to make a change and then follow through with their promise is not always an easy process. There is, however, a very powerful way to get individuals to choose the healthier behavior on their own. An exercise with which I've had very good results goes as follows:

(a) Ask the other person to consider carefully the way a particular behavior (assuming that it is negative and therefore a withdrawal from the relationship) has affected the relationship. Next ask them to write down what their relationship with you would look like in a year if this is not corrected…then in five years… and then ten… and eventually for the rest of their life.

One can imagine that the above-mentioned scenario gets increasingly darker as the years go by. Most people by the time they write the last part, (that being the rest of their lives), are quite depressed about the future of their relationship. This of course is the whole point of the exercise: to recognize how one uncorrected negative behavior can have a devastating effect on a relationship.

(b) Next ask the other person to consider what could happen to the relationship if this negative behavior were completely eliminated and replaced with a healthy, kind and loving one. The individual then writes down the results after a year…five years…ten…and for the rest of their life. The outcome of this scenario becomes more and more positive and uplifting as the years go by.

(c) Finally, ask the person to put these two documents side by side. Have them consider, "What will the rest of my life look like if I keep acting this way vs. if I eliminate the negative behavior and replace it with a positive behavior?" I actually have clients read these two documents out loud, back to back. The first brings about tears of sadness while the second one brings tears of joy. My final statement to them is, "You are looking at the future, written by your very own hand! Which will you choose?" I have never met anyone who said, "I'll choose to keep doing the same behavior…" It's usually, "Now that I've seen the potential destructiveness and the potential for growth and improvement, I can't wait to get started!"

4. The following is a fun exercise to do, particularly for your romantic relationship.

Ask your significant other/spouse to do this exercise at the same you're doing it. As described by Gary Chapman in his book, *The 5 Love Languages*, people express love in five different ways: 1) through words of affirmation, 2) by spending quality time together, 3) by giving gifts, 4) by performing acts of service, and 5) through physical touch. Each of you should divide a piece of paper into two columns. In the first column, make a list of the love languages in hierarchical order of their importance to you. Put the language that is most important to you at the top, and that which is least important to you at the bottom of the list.

In the second column, make a list of the love languages in hierarchical order of their importance to your partner. When you and your partner have both completed the exercise, compare your lists and discover whether you truly understand how your partner needs to be loved, and whether they really know how you need to be loved.

I've done this exercise with clients hundreds of times, and only one time was a couple able to identify each other's love languages in the correct order for each other! It was at a marriage seminar, and they were sitting right next to each other. I think they must have been cheating!

Chapter Ten
The Seventh Path: Serve From Your Heart.

Friend: "I think what you are doing is so great, to open up your home to him. Honey, you are changing that boy's life."
Leigh Anne Tuohy: "No, he is changing my life."
— From the 2009 movie "The Blind Side"

JOHN DONNE'S IMMORTAL POEM "NO MAN IS AN ISLAND" IS OFTEN quoted for its beautiful expression of the concept that we do not stand alone. We are each members of a great human family, and whether we realize it or not, we are all inextricably connected and bear responsibilities for one another. This point became clear very early in written history, after Cain killed Abel. When asked where his brother was, Cain tried to disavow responsibility as he arrogantly inquired, "Am I my brother's keeper?" The answer to that question is a resounding, "yes!"

The second great commandment is to "love your neighbor as yourself." And who exactly is your "neighbor?" *Everybody's* your neighbor.

Have you ever noticed how good it makes you feel to do something for another person, even if it's as simple as holding a door open for a stranger, or letting another car move into line ahead of you when heavy traffic is merging? Why is that? Why do we so revere a hero who gives his life to save another's?

As we lose ourselves in the service of others, we discover our own lives and our own happiness.
—**Dieter F. Uchtdorf**

It's a fundamental truth that we feel good when we put someone else first. One of the quickest ways to get out of the "funk" in which we may sometimes find ourselves is to lose ourselves in the service of somebody else, especially somebody who is having a tough time.

Providing Service Improves Our Character

One of my favorite mottos is "Ask not what others can do for you; ask what you can do for others." Mother Teresa of Calcutta had the following essay hanging on the wall of her convent. It has been said she adapted it from an essay written by Kent M. Keith:

> People are often unreasonable, irrational, and self-centered. Forgive them anyway.

Chapter Ten: The Seventh Path: Serve From Your Heart

If you are kind, people may accuse you of selfish, ulterior motives. Be kind anyway.

If you are successful, you will win some unfaithful friends and some genuine enemies. Succeed anyway.

If you are honest and sincere, people may deceive you. Be honest and sincere anyway.

What you spend years creating, others could destroy overnight. Create anyway.

If you find serenity and happiness, some may be jealous. Be happy anyway.

The good you do today will often be forgotten. Do good anyway.

Give the best you have, and it may never be enough. Give your best anyway.

In the final analysis, it is between you and God. It was never between you and them anyway.

—Mother Teresa

Mother Teresa exemplified these principles. For decades, she served the untouchables of India. She fed people who were not just hungry, but starving to death; she literally clothed the naked. She healed their wounds, both spiritually and emotionally. She never lost her focus on the people she was serving, even after she received the attention of the world. I'm not suggesting that we all need to go to the lengths Mother Teresa did, abandoning family, friends and a normal life to serve in the ghettos of Calcutta. But we can perform acts of kindness for others in the same humble way that Mother Teresa did.

> *Ask not what others can do for you;*
> *ask what you can do for others.*
> —**Unknown**

An interesting example of how service can change a person's character lies in the programs that allow prisoners to work on farms, caring for animals. It has been found that the service these hardened convicts provide gives them a whole new "lease on life." Most people who are in prison are there because of some selfish action, yet by losing themselves in service, the prisoners actually find themselves. This principle is embodied in the Bible where Jesus Christ said, "He that loses his life shall save it." (Luke 9:24.)

> *Service to others is the rent you pay*
> *for your room here on earth.*
> — **Muhammad Ali**

Have you ever been around somebody whose personality appears to be all about "me, myself and I?" Do they seem like they're truly happy? Interestingly, people who are incredibly selfish are sometimes very successful by the world's standards, but completely miserable on a personal level. I once had such a client. I'll call him "Jim." Jim had moved continuously up the corporate ladder of a big company until he reported straight to the CEO. He had a lot of responsibility, traveled all the time, and was financially very successful, yet his relationships were a disaster! He was very disconnected; his marriage was failing and his kids would not talk to him. Jim was really frustrated and angry. The first time I met with him, he confided in me, "I always thought that when I reached this position and made this much money, I'd be happy." But he realized that his life was actually quite empty. When we started to examine his situation, everything pointed to his self-centeredness. He hadn't invested any time in his relationships; his focus was all about himself, even when he was home. Sadly, when he was away traveling, there was more peace in the home and things ran a lot more smoothly.

Jim wanted to be happy. I asked him how he thought he was going to accomplish that — would it be through his next promotion, or the next raise? And he answered, "No, I've been there, done that, and it hasn't brought me happiness." I gently and gradually helped him to discover that he needed to turn his focus toward other people, and to serve them. But he didn't seem to know how to do that. One might think, "How could a person not know how to be of service to somebody else?" For whatever reason, some people just don't know how. Jim had been raised in a single-parent home, and at a young age he had to learn to rely on himself. He had decided he was "not going to be a loser like his dad," but in the process, he never learned that people are the most important part of life. He took them for granted; would buy them something extravagant when things were bad - but that wasn't what they needed. They needed his attention, his love, his time, and his service.

It wasn't an easy transition for Jim, because he was so used to thinking about himself. To his credit, he was a good guy underneath it all — just self-centered. It was a great thing for me personally to witness his transformation as he learned to work on the relationships that mattered to him. I gave him homework assignments that involved providing service to his family members. One was that he needed to do something for his wife every day until his appointment the following week. I told him, "You can't buy something, and you have to invest some time and energy and effort into it." He was really frustrated by the assignment. "Like what?!" he exclaimed. He just didn't know how to think that way, and I had to give him suggestions. I told him to go home, take his wife's car to the car wash, fill it up with gas, and then leave it in the garage for her. "Why?!" he asked, incredulous. I responded, "You won't know until you do it." He had to experience it for himself. You can tell somebody that if they serve somebody they'll feel good, but the person won't truly "get it" until they actually do it.

I also told Jim he needed to take his 16-year-old daughter on a date. Pick her up from school and take her on a lunch date. Before long, I had him going on date nights with each one of his kids. Initially, it was a little rough. When he first asked the kids to do something with him, they didn't want to, so he just blew them off and claimed that he had tried. "Well, you didn't try," I pointed out, "you only offered to do what YOU wanted to do. You have to do things with them that THEY want to do." Again, he gave me an incredulous look and wailed, "Like What? *WHAT* am I supposed to do with them?" "I don't know," I persevered, "that's why you have to talk to your kids! Find out what they like to do. Get interested in their lives."

He took his homework assignments seriously, and he did them. His family didn't know why he was working with me, and they thought something was really wrong. They even wondered if maybe he was dying. The kids all asked their mother, "What's wrong with Dad? He's acting weird!" (What a classic teenager response!) They didn't know what to make of it. The kids were able to experience their dad in a whole different way, and it drastically improved his relationships with them. He had always been too busy, too involved with work, or

Chapter Ten: The Seventh Path: Serve From Your Heart

had had better things to do. My reaction to that was, "Really? Better things to do than invest in your family?"

Jim was in his 40's, yet his life was transformed by performing such simple acts of service. In addition, other areas of his life improved; he became a better boss at work. It wasn't just about serving his wife and kids. He started thinking about his secretary, about the "little people" in the company – and essentially, he started being a nicer person. I asked him one day, "What's the last thing you did for your secretary?" and his response was, "What do you mean? She has a job!" His point was, he gave her a job, so what else could she need?! "When was the last time you asked her what her life was like?" I prodded. He answered, "Why? She's here to do a job, and I'm paying her." That week his assignment was to do something for his secretary. He belted out his usual response to me: "WHAT???? You're driving me crazy! Why do you want me to do this?" I told him to give her a gift certificate and then asked him what she liked. "I have no idea!" was his answer. "Why don't you find out?" I rejoined. When he asked "Why?" again, I said, "Just because it's the right thing to do. Just do it, and see what happens."

It was amazing to see the happiness, joy and peace that entered Jim's life. I think his wife had just been waiting for the kids to grow up so she could divorce him. He hadn't been unfaithful and he didn't have any addictions, but he wasn't very pleasant to be around. As he performed acts of service for the people he loved, Jim became more easy-going, his life was more in balance, and he was able to enjoy things more. He really struggled at first, because it was not second nature for him. But he did it anyway. If Jim was able to do it, I think anybody can do it.

Listen to Promptings

There was a time in my life when I felt like I was drifting, in surviving mode, and not really thriving. One day as I watched the news on television about a devastating earthquake in Haiti, I had a really strong feeling that I needed to do something about it. Typically when we watch something on the news, we think, "Oh, those poor people, that's terrible," then change the channel. Sometimes if we're really moved, we'll pick up the phone and donate some money to the cause. But this time I had a really strong prompting, almost a voice, that said, "You need to do something about this." And that began a journey over the following month that ended with my going to Haiti.

I believe that we all get messages like that on a daily basis. The important thing is whether or not we listen to those promptings. We might not hear them because we're not listening for them, or we may hear them and choose to ignore them. But when we hear and act upon those promptings, the results can be life changing, as my trip to Haiti was.

I contacted Dr. Terry Lyles, a friend of mine who's a nationally known expert on helping people who have been victims of a natural disaster, and I learned that he was also planning to travel to Haiti. We decided to go together, and I started writing articles in my weekly column about the upcoming trip. Before long, various people sent me information about the Foyer de Sion Orphanage in Port-Au-Prince, which needed help. Soon people were donating money and goods that we could take to the orphanage.

When we arrived in Haiti the conditions were absolutely awful, and involved everything that I dislike. There were enormous amounts of trash, noise, and dust; there was no running water, spotty electricity, inadequate food, and I had to sleep on the ground. Yet in the absence of any physical comfort and with very little sleep, I loved it! I loved serving the children in the orphanage. When I met them, they totally stole my heart! They were beautiful children, who amazingly, were still filled with light in the midst of tragic circumstances. Whenever we ventured out and returned to the orphanage, all 60 kids surrounded us and wanted to be picked up. Their need for physical affection and love was both heartbreaking and wonderful at the same time. We spent a lot of time with them, and that turned out to be one of the highlights of the trip. I completely lost myself in holding, loving and playing with them. I forgot that my back hurt from sleeping on the floor and I wasn't getting anything to eat except three energy bars and one big bottle of water a day. I've never been happier, while living in a place that was like being in the middle of Hell. It was bittersweet when I had to leave; I missed my family, having an actual meal, sleeping in a bed and taking showers. But if I had had 60 arms and could have held 60 kids at the same time, I would have done it. If I could have brought them all back home with me, I would have done that too. When you love and serve, the things that used to matter to you become secondary. And now I can't wait to go back – hopefully taking my family so they can experience that, too. Words don't do it justice.

We Love Whom We Serve

It's been said that we love those whom we serve. When we are kind and provide heartfelt service, we become friends with and even grow to love the people we serve. After spending a week in Haiti, I can understand why Mother Teresa never left the slums of India. She had discovered that the most meaningful work a person can ever do is doing something for somebody who has very little. The kids in the Haitian orphanage had nothing, yet they changed my life. They were full of joy! It was such a small thing to take the time to hold them - and I don't know what impact I had on them - but they had a tremendous impact on me.

A few years ago I became acquainted with a middle-aged woman who was taking care of her elderly father, who was rapidly declining in health. Throughout her life, they had had a difficult, sometimes even contentious, father-daughter relationship. There were periods in their lives when they didn't even speak to each other. But after his wife died, this daughter was the only family member who lived near him. He was alone, and as he aged, it fell to her to help him. She started to take care of him, driving him to his doctor's appointments, doing his shopping, and helping to clean his house. He continued to decline until he couldn't get out of the house anymore. The daughter then became his lifeline, and eventually, she had to completely care for him, bathing and even feeding him. Her devoted service continued for several years until the father passed away. Before this man's health had begun to fail, he had been intimidating to his daughter. Yet as she cared for him over the years, he declined to the point that he was completely dependent on her. No longer intimidating, he became more like a child. It was a very healing experience for both of them – she grew to love and even honor him.

Making a Difference Even to One Makes a World of Difference

In some ways, the world we live in is a sad, scary place where the needs of so many are so great, it may feel overwhelming when we contemplate trying to do something to help others. Yet we don't have to perform great or heroic deeds to reap the benefits that come from selflessly giving service to another. "The Star Thrower," a story in the work *The Unexpected Universe*, by Loren Eisley, beautifully illustrates this principle:

Once upon a time, there was a wise man who used to go to the ocean to do his writing. He had a habit of walking on the beach before he began his work. One day, as he was walking along the shore, he looked down the beach and saw a human figure moving like a dancer. He smiled to himself at the thought of someone who would dance to the day, and so, he walked faster to catch up. As he got closer, he noticed that the figure was that of a young man, and that what he was doing was not dancing at all. The young man was reaching down to the shore, picking up small objects, and throwing them into the ocean.

He came closer still and called out "Good morning! May I ask what it is that you are doing?"

The young man paused, looked up, and replied "Throwing starfish into the ocean."

"I must ask, then, why are you throwing starfish into the ocean?" asked the somewhat startled wise man.

To this, the young man replied, "The sun is up and the tide is going out. If I don't throw them in, they'll die."

Upon hearing this, the wise man commented, "But, young man, do you not realize that there are miles and miles of beach and there are starfish all along every mile? You can't possibly make a difference!"

At this, the young man bent down, picked up yet another starfish, and threw it into the ocean. As it met the water, he said "It made a difference for that one."[1]

> *To the world you may be just one person,*
> *but to one person you may be the world.*
> —**Unknown**

I was only 4 years old when the grandfather after whom I was named passed away. Yet in the short time I knew him, he gave me a very simple yet profound gift: I'll always remember him saying, "Just do something good every day."

He told me that I would have a successful life – be happier - if I made this world a better place than I found it. That principle has motivated me my entire life. We can each do that – we can change the world and make it a better place than we found it. It doesn't matter whether it's the world of one person at a time, or of a wider audience in one fell swoop. We can change the world of just one person, perhaps by helping their wounds heal, or by loving them, and by doing so we will have made this world a better place. And I have learned that doing so makes us happier. If we keep that thought as a guiding principle for each and every interaction that we have with other people, we will be happier, and we will definitely be making this world a better place.

There are countless ways in which we can give service, including making offerings to your church, or giving donations to a favorite charity. If you haven't practiced that in life, it can be a difficult adjustment to make, especially in difficult financial times. But it doesn't need to involve a large amount of money. If you see a homeless person, give them a quarter or a dollar, whatever you can spare. It's not going to "make or break" you, but it might make a world of difference to that person.

My wife Sona taught me this principle not long after we started dating. One weekend she invited me over to her apartment, and when I got there, she was making sandwiches. There were a lot of sandwiches – peanut butter and jelly, ham and cheese, tuna fish – and initially I thought she had invited me over to eat. I remember thinking, "I don't know if I can eat all that!"

> "What are you doing?" I inquired.
> "I'm just making sandwiches, do you want to help?"
> "What are they for?" I wondered.
> "I'm making them for the homeless. Every week I take them to a park in Santa Monica."

Of course I pitched in to help, because I wanted to make a good impression on her. But I had a stunning revelation when we arrived at our destination: the park was only a block from the apartment where I grew up. Santa Monica is a beautiful community, and there are a lot of homeless people there because of its wonderful weather. For years, I had ridden my bike past that park every day on my way to school. I had always felt uncomfortable – not in a judgmental way, but I was almost afraid of the homeless people who hung out in that park.

Sona gave me half of the sandwiches, but I was so uncomfortable about having any contact with those homeless men and women, I got rid of the sandwiches as quickly as I could, to the people who were nearby. Then I turned around, and realized that Sona was still with her first homeless person. She was kneeling down, had her hand on his shoulder, and as she gave him the sandwich, she made eye contact with him and talked with him. I was all done, and felt completely awkward because I didn't have anything left to give out. So for half an hour, I just followed her around from person to person like a lost puppy. Initially, I had just wanted to get done with the task, and it didn't even occur to me to focus instead on the people. When Sona was done with the last person, I saw the sun reflecting off her blonde hair, and that was when I fell in love with my wife. She looked golden – I saw her inner beauty as well as her outer beauty.

That experience was a defining moment in my life because being around homeless people had previously been far outside my comfort zone. As we drove home, I asked Sona, "What were you talking to them about?" She answered, "Most of these people feel invisible. Everybody walks by them, acts as if they don't exist. They treat them as if they were ghosts. But they're real people too; they're God's children too, and I just wanted them to know that they have value."

"Fast forward" to 20 years later, when one summer we went to California to visit family. We went to the beach, then to Disneyland, and had our fun. Everybody got to choose one thing they wanted to do on this vacation. And the activity my wife chose to do was to go to that same park and feed the homeless. The beauty of it was the impression it made on our kids. We went and did it her way – we both took one of our sons, and talked to each of the people to whom we gave a sandwich. When we got back in the car my younger son commented, "Man, if we lived here, I would want to do this every weekend." Our oldest son Niko a teenager, was so affected by the experience he was teary-eyed.

The blessing of giving service is that it transforms both people - the giver and the recipient.

Whether it's delivering Meals on Wheels or giving a buck to the guy on the street, we can all give something. No matter what our walk in life is, we can leave this world a better place than we found it. And in the process of doing so, we'll live in this world as a better, happier person. The blessing of giving service is that it transforms both people – the giver and the recipient.

It's not about convenience!

The Scouts have a saying: "Do a good turn daily" Which translates to, "do something for someone else, every day." It isn't "Do a good turn when it's convenient," or "When you feel like it;" it's "Do it *daily*" and regardless of whatever else is going on in your life. There's no question that people who perform some kind of service daily tend to be happier. You may already be doing this, and just not recognizing it. Mothers and wives give service every single day. If you're a parent who is actively involved with your children, there's no doubt that you perform service for others every single day.

Service often is *inconvenient*. Somebody might ask you to do something when you're tired, for example, but if you do it anyway, in my experience, you'll never regret it. In my church, we have opportunities to serve in different ways. One year, one of those opportunities was an assignment to work on a church-owned farm for a day. Food that is produced on the farm is kept in a church storehouse to aid families who are in need, and also donated to local community food banks. Having recently moved to the area, I wanted to make a good impression on the other members of my new congregation, so I volunteered to work on the farm for a day. I signed up in January, but the work wasn't to be done until June. As those six months passed, I totally forgot about the assignment. Then one Sunday in church came the announcement that everybody who had volunteered to work on the farm needed to meet at the church at 5:00 a.m. the following Saturday. An alarm went off in my head . . . "I'm doing what? What did I sign up for?!"

The following Saturday morning at 5:00 a.m. I found myself at the church, getting into a car, cursing the gods, and wondering why on earth I had volunteered for this! It was cold outside, we had to drive an hour to get to the farm, it was my one day off, and I wanted to be home in bed. When we finally got there, it was still cold out, and my attitude was bad as I continued to wonder what I had gotten myself into. I'm a total "city slicker." I grew up mostly in Athens, Greece and Santa Monica, California, and had never even been on a farm before. But everyone got to work, the sun came up, we began talking with one another, fellowship developed, and suddenly it was noon and time for lunch. The rest of the day passed quickly. I don't even remember what I did, but I'll never forget the warm feeling in my heart when we were driving back. I experienced a complete change in my perspective. At 5:00 am all I had thought was, "This is so stupid! What am I doing here?" But while driving home, I recognized that the happiest I've ever been in my life has been after giving service to others. Working on the farm that day was the last thing I had wanted to do, yet it ended up being as great a blessing to *my* life as it was to those who ultimately received the fruits of my labor.

Be People-Oriented Instead of Task-Oriented

The concept of providing service to others may not appeal to you because it seems like taking on extra work. But if you perform a service for another out of love, rather than out of a sense of duty, it won't feel like work!

The following is a beautiful story about a friendship that was truly enhanced by one who gave service:

Two Horses

Just up the road from my home is a field, with two horses in it. From a distance, each horse looks like any other horse, but if you stop your car, or are walking by, you will notice something quite amazing. Looking into the eyes of one of the horses you'll discover that he is blind. His owner has chosen not to have him put down, but has made a good home for him.

This alone is amazing. If you stand nearby and listen, you will hear the sound of a bell. Looking around for the source of the sound, you will see that it comes from the smaller horse in the field. Attached to the horse's halter is a small bell. It lets the blind friend know where the other horse is, so he can follow. As you stand and watch these two friends, you'll see that the horse with the bell is always checking on the blind horse, and that the blind horse will listen for the bell and then slowly walk to where the other horse is, trusting that he will not be led astray. When the horse with the bell returns to the shelter of the barn each evening, it stops occasionally and looks back, making sure that the blind friend isn't too far behind to hear the bell.

Like the owners of these two horses, God does not throw us away just because we are not perfect or because we have problems or challenges. He watches over us and even brings others into our lives to help us when we are in need. Sometimes we are the blind horse being guided by the little ringing bell of those who God places in our lives. Other times we are the guide horse, helping others to find their way. Good friends are like that. You may not always see them, but you know they are always there.

— Author unknown

We can each be the friend with the little bell. As true friends, we have a multitude of ways to serve and love others. In our overwhelmingly busy lives we can still create some quality time for those who could use our loving care. The key is to shift our thinking from being "task-oriented" to becoming "people-oriented." For those of us who are task-oriented, helping or spending time with people can be viewed as one of the jobs on our to-do list, something we rush through simply to get it done (like cleaning the house or grocery shopping). If we can change our way of thinking to allow the people in our lives to be our top priority - in other words, if we schedule time with people first, and then fill in necessary tasks with the time that is left, we will have a very different feeling about the services we perform for others. When we look back on our lives, which of those two things will we remember most? The relationships that we cherished, gave time and love to, or the time we spent accomplishing more tasks?

We're not generally raised to act that way. How do we put it into action? If we want to spend time with a child, spouse or an elderly parent, how do we incorporate that into our routine? Put it on the calendar! Writing it down as an appointment helps us to actually do it. If we need to go to the grocery store and our elderly grandmother lives nearby, we can visit her before going to the store. Not just show up, but also *really* spend time with her. Find out if there's anything she needs at the store, and get it for her. If walking is part of our daily routine, we can invite a family member or friend to be our walking buddy. Putting our relationships first will change our focus so that otherwise mundane chores instead become opportunities to enhance our connections with the people we care about.

Do it For the Right Reason!

We live in a very self-absorbed society. But the wonderful feelings we experience after providing service to someone aren't about being proud of ourselves. I knew a woman once – I'll call her "Sarah" - whose life motto seemed to be "What's in it for me?" When a friend of hers fell ill and was hospitalized, Sarah was asked to help the friend's husband, who was wheelchair-bound, for a couple of days. She took in dinner and helped him to get ready for bed both of those nights. She was so excited about having helped out, she talked about it constantly, wanting to be sure that all of her acquaintances knew that she had made huge sacrifices to help her friend. But Sarah didn't take away from the experience what she should have. She was so proud of herself, so busy bragging about what she had done, she was oblivious to the quiet, internal satisfaction and joy that come from selflessly serving somebody. If we "keep track" of what we're doing, then we're not giving from the heart. Our goal in giving service should not be to reap an eventual "payback" or to engender praise from other people.

There's an old saying I love that hangs on the wall of my office: "Blessed are those who give and forget, and blessed are those who receive and remember."

The Best Motivation

As was discussed in Chapter Two, most of the time people are motivated by pain, anger, fear (as in fear of the consequences if we don't do something), duty, or love. Love is the greatest of all motivators, and doing something out of love will usually result in greater happiness on the part of the giver. In regard to giving service, a sense of duty can also be a positive motivator. Doing something out of duty is not a bad thing; in fact, sometimes a person's motivation will change from a sense of duty to doing something out of love. When I went to Haiti, I went because of a feeling that I had a responsibility to do something. But as I experienced the joy of helping people there, my motivator was transformed to love, and the next time I go back, it will be because of the love I developed for the children in the orphanage.

> *Service is the action form of loving one another. When you truly love someone, you seek to serve them. Your concerns are for their happiness and welfare.*[2]
> —Lance Richardson

Service is Contagious!

Your actions may inspire others to do good. A wonderful example of this lies in the history behind an organization known as "Suitcases for Kids."

In November, 1995, 10-year-old Aubyn Burnside learned the average child in foster care moves three to four times and traditionally carries his/her personal belongings from home to home in black garbage bags. "I thought it was horrible that the children had nothing to carry their things in as they moved so many times. I wanted to make them feel special by giving them something of their own to keep. I tried to put myself in their place and think how I would feel," said Aubyn. Aubyn founded *Suitcases For Kids* in an effort to provide all 300 Catawba County [North Carolina] foster children with suitcases. She asked 4H-ers and Boy and Girl Scouts to help her. . . . [S]he asked [her church] as well as other churches to publish notices in their bulletins. She spoke to numerous Sunday School classes and put up posters at libraries, grocery stores and community buildings. The initial delivery of suitcases was 175 to Catawba County Department of Social Services in March 1996 . . . Within a month, suitcase deliveries had been made to social service departments in eight surrounding counties . . . . As the project spread through Scouting and 4-H networks, Aubyn ... began traveling to neighboring states to set up *Suitcases For Kids*. The project was featured in numerous newspapers and magazines nationwide. Aubyn appeared on the Oprah Winfrey Show and was named one of Oprah's Young Angels in her Angel Network. The project spread rapidly like a wildfire across America. At home, Aubyn received countless requests from volunteers in many states for information and advice on how to get the project started in their community. . . And by the end of its first full year, *Suitcases For Kids* was in operation in 19 states. Widespread awareness of Aubyn's project brought requests from many organizations. Russian children being brought to the U. S. for free medical and dental care needed luggage to carry home clothes, shoes, and gifts. Medical teams traveling to Bolivia, Mexico, Chili and Guatemala used suitcases to transport medical supplies into the countries. . . .Group foster home residents get suitcases for weekend visits back to their homes. Centers for unwed teenage mothers and their babies have depended on *Suitcases For Kids* for not only luggage but also diaper and baby bags. At the end of the second year, *Suitcases For Kids* was active in all 50 states and Canada and was being introduced into the Soviet Union . . . [By] its sixth year, *Suitcases For Kids* (www.suitcasesforkids.org) [was] an international nonprofit organization with chapters in every state as well as nine foreign countries.[3]

If a 10-year-old kid can inspire so many people, imagine what we can do if we put our hearts and minds to a worthy cause! Like Aubyn, once we've discovered the joy of providing service, we can spread that joy around. It's not hard to involve our children, friends, neighbors or co-workers. One of the great things about social media, whether it's through Facebook, Twitter or YouTube, is that it's possible to inspire millions of people, literally overnight. They also make it possible to spread happiness and joy throughout this often-troubled world in which we live. And teaching others about the joy of providing service is in and of itself an act of service.

Teaching the Joy of Service

We did service as a family on Christmas Day a few years ago that really made an impact on our children. On Christmas morning, after they opened their gifts, we all went to work at a family emergency assistance center for needy families in our county. People can go there and "shop" free for things they need, such as food, toiletries and other items. We went to a warehouse store, bought things for the assistance center, and stocked the shelves. As people literally came in off the streets, we were able to take them around to "shop." My children loved it, and we decided it was the greatest thing we had ever done for Christmas. It's something we'd like to make an annual tradition.

It's vitally important that we expose our kids to the joy of providing service, thereby helping them to experience what it feels like. That feeling isn't something that can be manufactured or bought. But it can be shared, and we can be an inspiration to others, motivating them to do good as they see us doing good.

It's worthwhile to note that recently there has been an increased focus in the media on people who help others. More and more television shows featuring extraordinary service by people to those who are less fortunate are being aired during prime time, such as "Extreme Makeover, Home Edition," "Secret Millionaire," and "Undercover Boss," and they are extremely popular. Many television stations now run awards programs such as the Denver NBC affiliate's "Nine Who Care," which honors people who give back to their communities by helping others. Even just *watching* other people give service to those who are less fortunate makes us feel good – imagine what you'll experience if you get involved in doing it yourself!

Giving Service Blesses Our Lives

Obviously, when we provide service to others our actions bless their lives. What is not so obvious is that doing so also brings *us* happiness and will bless *our* lives. Financial guru Suze Orman discovered this principle in the course of her career as an investment adviser. The author of multiple best-selling books on financial advice, Ms. Orman now counsels people to donate money to charity, because their financial situations will improve as a result. After a personal experience from which she learned that donating money to a good cause inevitably raised her spirits, she also discovered that any time she donated money to a charity, the amount she gave was ". . . showered back on [her] tenfold in no time."[4] She arrived at the conclusion that to be open to receive, people need to give to others. Following is an excerpt from *Suze Orman's Financial Guidebook*, in which she explains how she tested her new theory with her clients:

> I went back through my files and divided my clients into two groups, those who gave money [to charity] on a regular monthly basis and those who did not. What I found was that those who donated regularly had an abundance of money, more than they really needed. Most of the others didn't.
>
> To make sure my theory was correct, I did a little experiment with new clients who weren't doing so well with their money. I asked those I thought would be open to the idea to start donating money each month to a place they felt good about giving to. To new clients that in my opinion wouldn't be open to giving to

charity, I said nothing and just did their financial plans as normal. I couldn't believe the results. The better people felt about themselves from giving, and the more they kept their hands open to receive by relinquishing money, the more their financial situation improved. The key was to start respectfully to give money away by making an offering on a regular basis.[5]

Paying it Forward

Over the years, I have had the opportunity to work with hundreds of people who were battling addictions. Whenever I begin working with someone in this situation, I let them know that when they have overcome the addiction, not only will their lives become better, but the lives of those around them will improve, too. They will have the opportunity to help others.

A great illustration of putting this principle into action is the final step of the famous "twelve steps" program used by Alcoholics Anonymous. The 12th step involves doing some kind of service for others. Having had a spiritual awakening after practicing the first 11 steps, which are all about the addict, the person completing the program is required to go out and do something for somebody else as the final step. The program could stop at 11 steps – but it doesn't. Why the 12th step? It's the whole idea of "paying forward" the kindness that has been shown to the recovering addict. It involves practicing, in all of their affairs, the principles that have been learned through their spiritual awakening.

Isn't it interesting that the very last step, after all the healing has taken place, involves coming full circle? After being the recipient of other people's friendship and fellowship and help, the recovering addict is then in the position to become the fellowshipper and friend. *That's* a great example of becoming our "brother's keeper." As we have been helped, we can help others, and that "pay it forward" philosophy makes this world a better place. And in the end, isn't that what this life is all about? To leave this world a better place than we found it?

It has been said that when you are in the service of your fellow beings, you are only in the service of your God. And that's why it brings you happiness.

> *As you take the normal opportunities of your daily life and create something of beauty and helpfulness, you improve not only the world around you but also the world within you.*
> —**Dieter F. Uchtdorf**

Points to Ponder:

1. Service is the ultimate expression of love.
2. Service brings about change, to both the giver and the recipient
3. Service isn't always convenient
 . . . *but it's always worth it*

Questions to Consider:

1. Who can you serve today?
2. How can you make serving others a daily habit?

Take Action

1. Review your response to Question #24 in the Life Satisfaction Survey. If your answer was "sometimes," "rarely", or "never," that's an indication that service has not been a big part of your life. Since this is the only "Principle" that is focused outside of ourselves, it is vitally important for you to make service more of a priority, and you will be happier as a result.

2. When was the last time you did something out of love? What was it? Write it down. Do you remember how you felt? Write that down, too. How does it feel now, even as you're writing it down? It should bring back the warm feelings.

(a) What's the last thing you did out of love for someone?
_____

(b) How did you feel while you did it, and after it was done?
_____

3. Do something with love for somebody, and observe the difference it makes in how you feel when you do it, as well as how you feel afterward. Write down your plan for what you're going to do.

_____
_____
_____

(a) Write the name of a person for whom you want to do something.

_____

(b) What are you going to do for them?

_____

(c) When are you going to do it?

_____

4. Make a commitment to provide service in some way to someone on a monthly basis. Look for an opportunity to serve somebody you wouldn't normally serve.

Write down your plan for the first month:

_____
_____
_____
_____

CONCLUSION

As you read this book, you may have recognized a theme throughout many of the chapters: the happier you are, the more you will bless the lives of those around you. The more you bless the lives of those around you, the more you make this world a better place.

To Laugh often and love much;
To win the respect of intelligent people
And the affection of children;
To earn the appreciation of honest critics
And endure the betrayal of false friends;
to appreciate beauty;
to find the best in others;
to leave the world a bit better
whether by a healthy child,
a garden patch,
or a redeemed social condition;
to know even one life has breathed easier
because you have lived.
This is to have succeeded.
—Ralph Waldo Emerson

The Paths described in Chapters Three through Eight of this book focus on the things you may need to change about yourself to be happier. The Paths described in Chapters Nine and Ten focus on what you can do to bring happiness to others, thereby increasing your own happiness. **Spreading happiness to other people is what gives our lives meaning and makes us truly happy.** Living the principles discussed in this book consistently, until they become habits, can help you to live a happier life. The power of our personal habits is described well in one of my favorite poems:

Who Am I

You may know me . . . I'm your constant companion.
I'm your greatest helper, I'm your heaviest burden.
I'll push you onward . . . or drag you down to failure.
I am at your command if you choose to use me.
Half the tasks you do . . . can be turned over to me.
I'm able to do them quickly and I'm able to do them the same every time.
I'm easily managed – all you have to do is be firm with me.
Show me exactly how you want it done.
After a few lessons, I'll do it automatically.
I am the servant of all great men and women.
And of course, the servant of all the failures as well.
I've made all the great individuals who have ever been great,
And all the losers, too.
I work with the precision of a computer
And the intelligence of a human being.

You may run me for profit, or you may run me to ruin . . .
It makes no difference to me.
Take me. Be easy with me and I will destroy you.
Be firm with me and I'll put the world at your feet.
Who am I?
I am your Habit.

—Author Unknown

It's my hope that you, dear reader, will be able to successfully incorporate into your life the principles described in *7 Paths to Lasting Happiness* until they become habits for you. One of the greatest accomplishments of life is to leave this world a better place than we found it. We can do that by making a positive difference in the life of another person. Sharing happiness is about blessing the lives of other people. It's about spreading the "light" to whatever sphere of influence we have. If this book results in just one person living a happier life, then it will have been a huge success. I hope that your life will be blessed with much joy, happiness and laughter.

Sincerely,

—*Dr. Elia Gourgouris*

CHAPTER NOTES

Chapter One.

1. Seymour, Liz. "A Formula for Happiness." *U.S. Airways Magazine* September, 2007. pp.67-70.

2. *Ibid.*, p.68.

3. Gilbert, Elizabeth. *Eat, Pray, Love.* Penguin Books. New York. 2006. p.260.

4. Seymour, p.68.

5. Elias, Marilyn. *USA Today.* "Study Links Sense of Humor, Survival." March 13, 2013. http://usatoday30.usatoday.com/tech/science/discoveries/2007-03-13-humor-study_N.htm. Accessed April 2, 2014.

Chapter Two

1. Roosevelt, Eleanor. *This is My Story,* New York, London: Harper & Brothers, 1937.

2. Gourgouris, Elia, Ph.D. and Marcucci, Jenner. "Life Satisfaction Survey," www.theHappinessCenter.com.

Chapter Three.

1. Haden, Jeff. "*7 Things Remarkably Happy People Do Often.*" April 21, 2014.

https://smallbusiness.yahoo.com/advisor/7-things-to-do-that-will-make-you-happier-175823605.html, April 23, 2014.

2*Ibid.*

Chapter Four.

1. Lyles, Dr. Terry, PhD. *Good Stress: Living Younger, Longer. Healthful Communications.* Juno Beach, Florida. 2006. pp. 90-92.

2. *Ibid*, p.59.

3. *Ibid*, pp.62-63.

4. Rumi, "Insomnia Treatment," March 10, 2010. http://treat-insomnia.com/sleep- deprivation/sleep-deprivation-statistics/.

5. Moon, Shawn. On Your Own: *A Young Adult's Guide to Making Smart Decisions.* Cedar Fort Publishing and Media, Springville, UT 2009.

Chapter Five.

1. Ten Boom, Corrie. *The Hiding Place.* Peabody, Massachusetts. Hendrickson Publishers. 2009.

2. Osteen, Joel. "Today's Word with Joel and Victoria," October 28, 2013. www.joelosteen.com/pages/messageviewer.aspx?

3. Gilbert, Elizabeth. *Eat, Pray, Love.* Penguin Books. New York. 2006. Pp. 178-179.

4. *Ibid.*

5. marcandangel.com. "30 Things to Stop Doing to Yourself.", http://www.lifebuzz.com/just-stop/#!3scCl, January 10, 2014.

Chapter Six.

1. Holman, Marianne quoting Dr. Frank Fincham in "Forgiveness in Marriage," The Church News, Week of March 3, 2013.

2. Chapman, Gary. *The 5 Love Languages*. Northfield Publishing. Chicago. 2010. P. 44.

3. Holman, quoting Dr. Frank Fincham.

4. *Ibid.*

5. *Ibid.*

Chapter Seven.

1. Mays, Jeff. "99-Year-Old Ghanaian Man Graduates College." April 5, 2010. http://www.bvblackspin.com/2010/04/05/99-year-old-graduates-college/?icid=main|compaq-laptop|dl5|link6|http%3A%2F%2Fwww.bvblackspin.com%2F2010%2F04%2F05%2F99-year-old-graduates-college%2F

2. Ditzler, Jinny. *Your Best Year Yet*. Warner Books, New York, 1994.

3. Uchtdorf, Dieter. "A Matter of a Few Degrees." *Ensign, A Magazine of the Church of Jesus Christ of Latter-Day Saints*, May 2008.

4. Pauley, Jane. *Your Life Calling: Reimagining the Rest of Your Life*. Simon & Schuster. New York, 2014. p. 243.

5. *Ibid.*, p.112.

6. Ditzler, pp. 35-36, 47-48, and 122.

Chapter Eight.

1. Coleman, Brenda C. "Heart Patients Who Are Prayed For Fare Better, Study Finds." Associated Press. October 1999. The Boston Globe's "Boston.com." http://www.boston.com/news/daily/25/heart_prayer.htm. August 15, 2013.

Chapter Nine.

1. Chapman, Gary. *The Five Love Languages*. Northfield Publishing, Chicago. 2010.

2. Powell, John. *The Secret of Staying in Love*. Niles, Ill.: Argus, 1974, p. 68.

3. Ashton, Marvin J. "Family Communications." *Ensign*. April 4, 1976.

Chapter Ten.

1. Eisley, Loren. *The Unexpected Universe*. Harcourt Brace & Company, Orlando, Florida. 1994.

2. Richardson, Lance. *The Message*. American Family Publications, Idaho Falls, Idaho. 2000. p. 117.

3. www.suitcasesforkids.org.

4. Orman, *Suze*. *Suze Orman's Financial Guidebook*. Three Rivers Press. New York. 2002. p. 159.

5. *Ibid.*, pp. 159-160.

Made in the USA
San Bernardino, CA
05 March 2016